D0759177

SYSTEMS DESIGN &
DEVELOPMENT CORP.

Software Metrics

WINTHROP COMPUTER SYSTEMS SERIES
Gerald M. Weinberg, *editor*

CONWAY AND GRIES
An Introduction to Programming: A Structured Approach Using PL/1 and PL/C-7, Second Edition

CONWAY AND GRIES
Primer on Structured Programming Using PL/1, PL/C, and PL/CT

CONWAY, GRIES, AND ZIMMERMAN
A Primer on PASCAL

GELLER AND FREEDMAN
Structured Programming in APL

GILB
Software Metrics

GILB AND WEINBERG
Humanized Input: Techniques for Reliable Keyed Input

Future Titles

CONWAY, GRIES, AND WORTMAN
Introduction to Structured Programming Using PL/1 and SP/k

ECKHOUSE AND SPIER
Guide to Programming

FINKENAUR
COBOL for Students: A Programming Primer

GELLER
Structured Programming in FORTRAN

GREENFIELD
The Architecture of Microcomputers

TOPPING
Simula Programming

WEINBERG, GOETZ, WRIGHT, AND KAUFFMAN
High Level COBOL Programming

WILCOX
Introduction to Compiler Construction

Software Metrics

Tom Gilb

Foreword by Gerald M. Weinberg

Winthrop Publishers, Inc.
Cambridge, Massachusetts

Library of Congress Cataloging in Publication Data

Gilb, Tom.
    Software metrics.

    Bibliography: p.
    Includes index.
    1. Computer programs — Evaluation. 2. Computer
programs — Reliability. I. Title.
QA76.6.G55   001.6'425'0724   76-40163
ISBN 0-87626-855-6

© 1977 by Tom Gilb
          Iver Holtersvei 2
          N-1410 Kolbotn
          Norway
          Telephone: (47 2) 80 16 97

Copublished by Studentlitteratur, Sweden

10 9 8 7 6 5 4 3 2 1

DEDICATED

TO

All the people who have patiently tried to explain to me why it was
"impossible", "impractical" or "uneconomic" to measure software
"quality",

and to my sons,

Dag Philip, Tor Steven, Kai Thomas and Per Bernhard.

I hope they won't listen to such nonsense either,

even from their father.

Contents

Part II: Metric concepts   129

List of illustrations and tables

Fig.

Fig.

LIST OF ILLUSTRATIONS IN PART II: METRICS CONCEPTS

REABILITY METRICS ILLUSTRATIONS

Fig.

Preface

This is the first book, as far as I know, to attempt to describe the emerging technology of software metrics. *

As such, I have had few examples to build on, and have felt very alone during the preparation of the text. In desperation, a lot of technology has been borrowed ("technology transfer") from system engineers, for whose guidance I am extremely grateful.

I hope that the essence of this text will not easily become obsolete. Yet I should consider it an honor if the book was replaced by texts which offered a better pedagogical approach, more solidly based concepts, and a larger collection of measuring examples and theoretical concepts. I expect this book to be a milestone, but hope it does not become a temple.

In such a pioneer work, I ask the reader's indulgence for some of the terms I have had to create, for some of the opinions expressed, and for the way the material is organized. Please accept it in the positive spirit of making use of what is useful and ignoring what is not.

Most of Part II (Metric Concepts) was written in the summer of 1972, and it was added to and nurtured over the next three years. I found that the subject matter was "stable", which means I didn't feel like throwing it away every year and trying again. I found that I was continually making use of the metric concepts as a consultant and writer, and that they therefore might be worth sharing with others. A reviewer for a publisher remarked that while he liked what he saw in this part, he didn't see any proof of the practical application of the concepts, and was skeptical. My first reaction was that he couldn't be very well read in the state of the art, but later I began to discover that a lot of my professional colleagues, for whom I have the highest regard, were mostly unaware of the practical application of metrics, and were even highly skeptical as to their practicality.

---

* The TRW Systems publication Characteristics of Software Quality is the only remotely comparable work. It is a step-by-step research report which tries to develop the art of software metrics. It is discussed later in this text in several places. My own work, published earlier the same year, described about 13 reliability-oriented metrics, but, as stated there, I only attempted to scratch the surface.

During the long evenings of the sunny summer of 1975, after taking a dip and a sail in one of the beautiful Norwegian fjords, I added the first part of this book (Practical Applications) so that readers would be in no doubt as to the practicality of metrics. It strikes me now that this first part may be regarded as the most worthwhile and interesting part of the book.

Foreword

"To measure is to know." So said James Clerk Maxwell, who more than any other converted electromagnetism from an amusement of the rich to a science serving humankind.

Not that any fool with a meter stick is a scientist. Maxwell might have continued, "To know *what* to measure is to know," or "To know *when* to measure — and when not to measure—is to know." These are the concerns of *Software Metrics:* how measure, what to measure, when to measure, and when to cease measuring and start building software.

Leonardo da Vinci had many ideas on the subject of measurement. For instance,

> When you wish to measure the breadth of a river, withdraw from its bank
> to a somewhat greater distance than the width of the stream and observe some
> fixed mark on the opposite bank of the river.

To gain some measure of the significance of *Software Metrics,* we would be wise to follow Leonardo's advice. The software river is wide and swift—if not exceptionally deep—and by standing too close we lose perspective and become confused by the turbulence.

In many and diverse societies, the biological transition from childhood to adolescence is accompanied by a cultural transition—a rite of passage. I believe that the publication of Tom Gilb's *Software Metrics* is part of a public maturation ritual for the art and science of software development.

To call software development an "infant" discipline is not a moral judgment, but merely a colorful way to summarize its short history and present existence. Every science or engineering discipline has an infancy, marked by symptoms as obvious to the experienced eye as the playful inquisitiveness of a puppy. We do not know if every field has a similar maturity, but in those that do, the maturity is marked by the ability to measure. However, until now software people have feared and resisted measurement in much the same way a child fears and resists the inevitable signs of growing up.

Why should we have misgivings about measurement?

I have written elsewhere of the sort of person attracted to computing in our infant years—often an individual seeking the certainty of machines to replace the higgledly-piggledy of people. The vital essence of the computer is that epitome of precision and certainty—counting.

Although never having done so, the child of five is certainly capable of counting to 1,000. When unable to sleep, adults count sheep until Morpheus wafts them away —we can relax in the certain knowledge that the counting will go on without us.

However, if integers are the morphine of numbers, floating point numbers—the representations of measurements—are the amphetamines. According to Bertrand Russell, we are reasonably certain that Cleopatra had one nose and two eyes—not, heaven forbid, 0.999998 noses and 2.000001 eyes. Pascal (another philosopher–mathematician enamored of the integers) once remarked, "Had Cleopatra's nose been shorter, the entire appearance of the earth would have been changed." Such a crucial nose, yet we do not even know its precise length. Dare we entrust the fate of the earth to such imprecisions? Dare we entrust the fate of our software projects to statisticians, historians, engineers, and other measurers? Why can we not stick to the integer facts of our programs, which are either right or wrong?

The answer is simple. Although the two possibilities are "right" and "wrong," actually we have not realized the "right" in practice. Once we do—if we do—there will be many other attributes to the quality of a program, qualities we must measure if we are to improve our performance.

We dread destroying the "beauty" of our software by attempting to measure what has heretofore been intuitive. The danger is genuine—we will never capture the beauty of a rose in floating point. However, we will not capture it in integers either. Moreover, beauty is not singular, but manifold. Gaze upon the Acropolis; rest in the shade of the Great Pyramid; encompass Paris from the Eiffel Tower. Under the artist's command, measurement becomes the servant of beauty.

But what happens to the artist? There remains an apprehension that once we have learned to measure, today's artist/superprogrammer will become a clerk. For a Pythagorean to reveal that $a^2 + b^2 - c^2$ meant death by torture. Yet today numerous schoolchildren know the Pythagorean theorem. The devaluation of specific information is both the price and the reward of progress in measurement. To remain the master, the artist must keep moving and try not to freeze and hoard knowledge. Few lessons of history are writ more clear: frozen knowledge does not keep.

According to the anthropologist Arnold Van Gennep, most rites of passage contain three phases: separation (from the old ways), segregation (in which the individual initiates are isolated from one another and from others), and integration (in which the neo-adult is brought back into society in the new role). With respect to measurement, computing has been undergoing *segregation* in that many individual workers and teams have struggled with questions of measurement in isolation from one another. In the earliest stages, such segregation is important if we are not to suppress the full flowering of ideas, but eventually we gain more from combining our ideas with those of others, as Tom Gilb has done.

Software Metrics marks a *separation* from the old ways—it announces, in public, a change in thinking which can never be reversed. It also begins the third phase, *integration,* although much remains to be done. The experiments, the concepts, and the metric values tabulated in *Software Metrics* are but a hint of the adult body of knowledge to come. In 10 years no more than 20 percent of the material will be recognizable, just as the child–adolescent is barely recognizable in the mature adult.

In 10 years, if *Software Metrics* succeeds, readers will say, "But most of this is obvious and inevitable. How else *could* it be?" Not that it is obvious or inevitable today. On each page, the reader will confront the immaturity of pet ideas, prejudices, and myths.

In reviewing my own notes, I find the entire spectrum of emotional response—shock, amusement, agreement, outrage, ridicule, disbelief, doubt, stimulation. Readers who have experienced Tom Gilb's seminars will recognize this emotional bath. I am amazed that so much of his unique style of communication could be captured in a different medium.

Like his seminars, Tom's book will quickly repay the cost of admission. Any one of a hundred ideas in *Software Metrics* will be worth the cover price to the data processing manager, the practicing programmer, the systems analyst or designer, and the professor or student of computer science—such is the power of his ideas.

But the power of ideas is essentially a *neutral* power. The best idea can be a force for good or a force for evil. To some readers, measurement is a method of squeezing the last gram of humanity out of the computing business. If *Software Metrics* leads to something like a Taylorian "scientific management" in software development, I for once, will bow my head in shame.

What can prevent this kind of dehumanizing application of metric ideas? Some social philosophers claim that nothing will avail, for dehumanization is an inevitable consequence of capitalist, socialist, communist, fascist, bureaucratic, elitist (pick one or more) systems. However, if it is inevitable our actions do not matter, so we might as well follow measurement wherever it leads.

Another view, more compatible with my own philosophical prejudices, says that individual efforts *do* matter. What one person does—what *I* do—to humanize or dehumanize may be but a few teardrops in the ocean, but it does matter. It matters because it *will* make a difference if we start believing it does not matter—and dehumanization will then be inevitable. I believe that *Software Metrics* was written with a deep feeling of the importance of each individual's efforts to build a better, more mature, more responsible discipline of software development and use. Now you hold that responsibility in your own hands.

—Gerald M. Weinberg

Introduction to the subject matter of software metrics

"... the measure you give will be the measure you get, and still more will be given to you." (St. Mark 4:24)

Man´s victories over nature, in science and engineering, are closely correlated with his ability to measure whatever he is working with. This is related to the ability to recognize and measure all the critical factors involved. In many cases the accuracy of the measuring instrument itself has been the critical factor in a new development.

It seems obvious that software, in the broadest sense of the word (i. e. all "non-hardware" parts of computerized systems) is at a point where we are moving from a handicraft into an engineering industry, with a corresponding scale and degree of risk involved. We have had just enough large failures in software projects to motivate us to acquire full control over our technology.

We must measure what we are doing, and in particular we must measure the critical factors, and not simply the easily available ones, such as space and time consumption, which have been the major area of computer measurement so far. In particular, the measures relating to the use of human talent resources (for example maintainability and portability) are becoming of major interest owing to their high cost and scarcity today, compared to the comparatively cheap machine resources.

Measures related to reliability of function are becoming more important as we dare to use computers for increasingly crucial functions.

The reader should be able to enjoy reading about the practical applications of metrics in Part I, whether he is a student or a mature computer professional. The metric concepts in Part II can be studied formally by students, and I hope that practitioners in the field will at least scan the contents in preparation for later reference, when they have the technical specifications in the software contract in front of them, and need some stimulation for what and how to specify particular qualities that they are responsible for evaluating.

Finally, I hope that this text will be useful as a counter-argument to those who are skeptical of the applicability of a wide range of metrics to software, and proof that there are reasonable theoretical, practical and economically viable ways of measuring all critical software concepts.

I hope that no reader will ever feel limited by whatever happens to be contained in this text. It is only a reflection of the limitations of the author and of the point in time at which the text was written.

The spirit in which this book was written is that all critical software concepts have at least one practical way of being measured. It may not be elegant, but if it improves results, it should be used until perfectionists can indicate a better tool.

I hope that this text will provide common terms of reference for describing the results and experiences encountered by my readers, in more objective and more precise language.

I trust that the reader will agree that the attempts to spread software religions, such as those of the last few years regarding "data bases" and "structured programming", that have not provided objectively measurable results, are not worthy of attention, and deserve to be challenged as any other science or engineering discipline would demand that they be.

This text gives the reader a systematic checklist of measures which can be made of interesting software phenomena, and a reasonable picture of practical and economical ways of determining the value of the measure in question at any point in the development of the software.

Armed with this body of information, the reader has no excuses for not using metrics and is forced to make use of this technology or provide a better one.

If even the immediate past of software metrics is any guide, many a useful measure and many a useful measuring tool will continue to be invented. Unfortunately only a few of these inventions will be permanently recorded, and so they will be lost to the rest of us, perhaps to be reinvented by still others again.

Readers who find no other way of spreading their metrics experiences should know that I should be pleased to receive information about any such experiences which they wish to share with the rest of us.

A broad definition of software

In the minds of many practitioners of computer arts, the word "software" tends to have a limited meaning.

In the narrowest sense of the word it means general utility programs such as operating systems, compilers, data base management programs and the like. Many will immediately be willing to include all sorts of other programs, there being really only an arbitrary borderline between such utility programs and any other class of program.

Some, when pressed, will admit that there are things like tables of values and files upon which the programs might be dependent for their correct operation, and that this data is somehow also software.

If we look at the word itself, soft ware, it is clearly intended to contrast with the term hardware, which was all that many early computers (and even some present microcomputers and some early minicomputers) consisted of.

I submit the obvious, that software is quite simply all the non-hard components required to make a computerized system function effectively.

Using this broad definition one can immediately list a number of things that many people would find hard to accept. Is the "motivation" that is consciously designed into a computer application also "software", for example? Personally, I believe it is (see ' Motivational Factors') but I am not willing to labor the point for the skeptical reader.

I have based my thesis on the following assumption:

> Software is composed of two major components:
> a. logicware, which is the logical sequence of instructions controlling the execution sequence done by the hardware, and
> b. dataware, which is the physical form in which all information, including logicware, appears to the hardware, and which is processed as a result of the logic of the logicware.

I believe that in spite of the fact that the widely used term "data processing" implies a clear recognition of the equal importance of both the dataware and the logicware which processes it, we have too long neglected to study the role of dataware in limiting (or creating opportunities for) the programmer in the algorithms he can use. I shall deal briefly with this belief and with the basis for it later in the text.

The recent emergence of the study of data and data design techniques will have a profound effect on the thinking and the training of programmers and program designers. In time, dataware will be considered at least as important a study as logicware is today.*

In the meantime, the tools presented in this text should serve to promote this recognition, and they should not be made obsolescent by the emergence of the dataware technology. Therefore software, in this text, means the dataware and logicware systems which we are interested in designing, analyzing or describing.

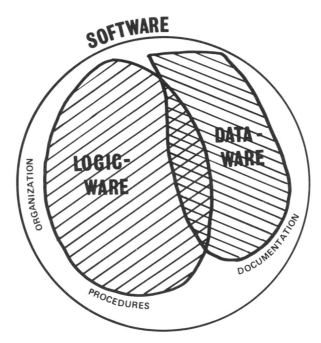

Fig 1. Software is a broad systems concept embracing all non-hard elements of the system. The two principal software elements are LOGICWARE (the active instructions which direct the processing of the data) and DATAWARE (the passive data which gets interpreted and changed by the logicware).

* See other books by this author (Data Engineering, Humanized Input)

18

LEVELS OF SOFTWARE

As we can see from Fig 2, the world of software has grown increasingly complex. It is clearly beyond the capabilities of any individual to fully understand the practical consequences of a total working set of software by merely reading the program listings (as was possible a dozen years ago and is still possible with more primitive systems today). It is therefore becoming important that we develop more sophisticated ways of measuring the functional parts of these complex systems and of adding the qualities of individual parts and levels of the systems, so as to describe any cumulative part of the system in a meaningful fashion.

SEVEN LEVELS OF PROGRAMS BETWEEN THE USER AND THE HARDWARE

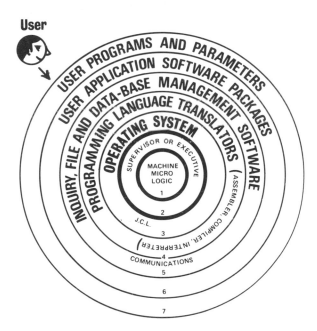

Fig 2. Logicware and associated dataware have become increasingly complex. We cannot expect specialists to derive software attributes from functional descriptions of the software. A "black box" approach must be used to describe the attributes of software components.

METRICS

The problem is not new. It has been encountered in many rapidly growing disciplines. When structural description is no longer adequate to fulfill the practical demands for understanding complex systems, a new language must be found, which will describe the interesting attributes of the system in terms that are independent of the structure which leads to these attributes. I have called this language metrics, which simply means measures. It involves a set of measures that are quantified numerically and have useful accuracy and reliability.

The object of this book is first to explore the practical developments and uses of software metrics as they exist today, at the edge of the state of the art, and secondly to give the reader a systematic collection of metrics concepts - not a final one, but hopefully a good start.

PART I

Practical applications of software metrics

Introduction - practical methods for measuring various software metrics concepts

There are two important stages in software property measurement:

- agreement on the measuring concept (the "volt")

- finding a sufficiently economical and accurate tool for measuring the property in a real system (the "voltmeter")

Opinions on how to express measuring concepts and on which metrics are the most important ones to check will always differ, but some dominating metric concepts will tend to emerge and remain stable, accepted concepts for a longer period of time, on a survival of the fittest basis.

However, even where there is a stable metric available for some interesting system property, the measuring instruments will tend to be varied, tailor-made to fit the system, and constantly changing as the years pass.

This high rate of change in the measuring instruments, which can be observed in all scientific, engineering and business applications, is probably attributable to the following factors:

- the need for greater accuracy of measurement

- the need for more reliable measuring

- the need for more economic measuring

- the invention or development of instruments which satisfy the above needs

- differences in the applications being measured.

The following examples of measuring techniques are not intended to be a complete set of recommended measuring instruments.

The state of the art is developing so rapidly at this point that it is unlikely that any such text could present the best possible methods for software metric measurement. In fact the reader should be largely prepared to develop his own measuring instruments for particular applications, and to use the following examples as a guide.

PREDICTING THE RELIABILITY OF A PROGRAM BEFORE IT IS TESTED, AND CONFIRMING IT

TRW-Systems performed an interesting experiment in reliability measurement (TRW-SS-74-14, pp. 5-30/33).

Based on the intuition that reliability is related to the program complexity and the program documentation, two programs written by different programmers, based on the same program specifications, were evaluated.

Program A was written in a simple straightforward manner by an engineering-oriented programmer, while program B was written by a "hotshot" programmer and was full of "loops and programming tricks".

Based on certain criteria (see TRW-SS-73-09 for details) of complexity and documentation, the following reliability estimates were made:

Program A   (simple)   95. 8%
Program B   (exotic)   89. 3%

The two programs were then subjected to a test of 1000 sample inputs based on an operational profile of the program, which were selected with a random number generator. The percentages of correctly executed cases for the two programs were:

Program A   99. 7%   (a priori prediction 95. 8%)
Program B   96. 3%   (a priori prediction 89. 3%)

The pre-testing metric managed to predict that the simple program would be more reliable.

The "exotic" program, by the way, took just as much storage and run time as the simpler program.

SOFTWARE MAINTENANCE

(Hoskyns Survey: 905 British Installations)

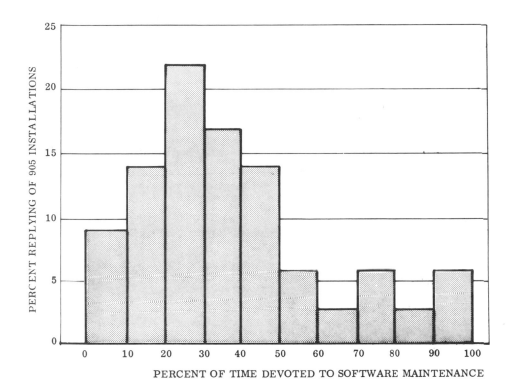

Fig 3. Software maintenance effort is a substantial cost in most computer
installations and the burden increases with time. In addition to
maintenance of operational programs the creation of new programs
requires a substantial debugging effort (around 50%, see Fig 45)
which itself is dependent on the program quality called "maintainability": It is therefore of great importance that we make use
of techniques for specifying and measuring maintainability.
Source: reprinted in Boehm's paper (THCOS-73)

Maintainability measurement and the bebugging technique

Software maintainability measurement

How can one measure computer program maintainability? The metric concept is simple enough, and it is a stable concept which is widely accepted by engineers.

Maintainability is the probability that, when maintainance action is initiated under stated conditions, a failed system will be restored to operable condition within a specified time. (see "Metric Concepts: Maintainability").

In a real system, a reasonable practical estimate of the degree of maintainability can be derived from job report statistics of maintenance programmers. If, say, 100 program repairs have been effected and the time needed to do them has been noted, then some sort of curve can be drawn indicating the different probabilities of repair within certain time limits.

This is historical data, and the sample size and controlled conditions will not be adequate for all purposes, but the "maintainability" of that program under those conditions has most certainly been measured. The only thing to be discussed is whether or not the accuracy and reliability of the measure is adequate for our particular purposes.

If for example our purpose is to monitor the "maintainability" quality of a real program to see whether it is still meeting design specifications, the measure may be quite adequate. Say that the original design specification was that "95% of all program bugs which cause serious problems can be repaired successfully within one hour" (which is an informal, but still a practical and interpretable specification). Our measure of the first 100 bugs repaired (we assume they were serious otherwise why bother to repair them?) shows that the maximum time for the repair of the 95 most quickly repaired bugs was 50 minutes. The average repair time was 30 minutes and the worst single repair time was 10 hours. I would say that the program has a maintainability which satisfies specifications.

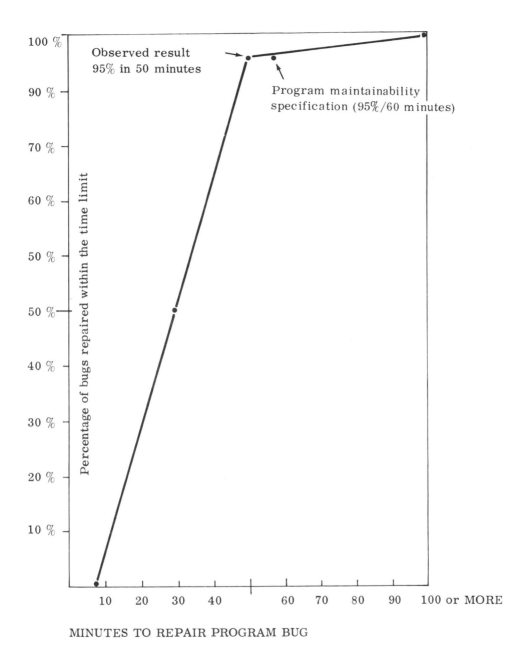

Fig 4. A hypothetical maintainability curve based on the data in the
example given in the text.

Contracts with maintainability measures

The above example is simplified, but this kind of measurement is very close to the kinds of measures that have been applied for many years in connection with well-written contracts involving systems with a software component. In these contracts, if a computer is inoperable for <u>any</u> reason (hardware or software) due to a vendor-supplied product, then the failure period, until repair is effected, is written in logs and penalties may be extracted from vendors who use too long a time to repair the software.

"Error correction during the warranty period should always specify the 'turnaround time' for repairs, i.e., the responsiveness required of the vendor in repairing user-detected errors, particularly errors which jeopardize the buyer's ability to perform the tasks for which he bought the software." (BERNACCHI 73-20889, p. 355, in discussing software contracts).

The bebugging method of maintainability measurement

A method which I call "bebugging" (GILB-750401), but which Harlan Mills of IBM describes as "inspection statistics ... based on the intentional, but random, seeding of errors in a program in order to calibrate the error finding process itself" (p. 236 in HETZEL-73), can be used for a more highly controlled study of the maintainability of software.

John D. Gould and Paul Drongowski of IBM Research and Carnegie-Mellon University respectively have used the insertion of artificial bugs into a source program as a means of measuring the effects of different aids for improving the maintainability of a source program. Fig 5 shows one of several source programs which they used in their experiment, and gives an indication of the kinds of bugs they inserted, one at a time.

Results of a maintainability measuring experiment

The following table (Fig 6) shows a selection of the results of using the artificial bug insertion method in an effort to determine which documentation helps programmers find bugs correctly and most effectively.

The randomly selected individual programmers in each group were stopwatch-timed as they searched for each artificial bug. Each group of individuals had different "hints" (documentation) about the bug:

A BEBUGGED PROGRAM. 3 BUGS INSERTED.

```
C                                                                    TALL  10
C      .........................................................TALL  20
C          PURPOSE OF PROGRAM                                        TALL  50
C              TO CALCULATE TOTAL,MEAN,STANDARD DEV., MINIMUM, MAXIMUM TALL  70
C              FOR EACH VARIABLE IN A SET (OR A SUBSET) OF OBSERVATIONS TALL  80
C      .........................................................TALL  85
C          INSTRUCTIONS TO SUBJECTS                                  TALL  77
C              ASSUME AN OBSERVATION MATRIX,NO X NV.  NO = NUMBER OF  TALL  90
C              OBSERVATIONS = 30, AND NV = NUMBER VARIABLES = 20.  ASSUME TALL 100
C              THESE SCORES ARE CORRECTLY READ INTO CORE IN A VECTOR, TALL 110
C              A(1) - A(600).                                        TALL 120
C              S(1)-S(30) = INPUT VECTOR INDICATING SUBSET OF A. ONLY TALL 150
C                  OBSERVATIONS WITH A NON-ZERO S(J) ARE CONSIDERED.  TALL 160
C                  VECTOR LENGTH IS NO.                              TALL 170
C              TOTAL(1)-TOTAL(20) = OUTPUT VECTOR OF TOTALS OF EACH VAR. TALL 180
C              AVER(1)-AVER(20) = OUTPUT VECTOR OF AVER'S OF EACH VAR. TALL 200
C              SD(1)-SD(20) = OUTPUT VECTOR OF STD. DEVS. OF EACH VAR. TALL 220
C              VMIN(1)-VMIN(20) = OUTPUT VECTOR OF MINIMA OF EACH VAR. TALL 260
C              VMAX(1)-VMAX(20) = OUTPUT VECTOR OF MAXIMA OF EACH VAR. TALL 280
C      .........................................................TALL 450
C                                                                    TALL 460
       DIMENSION A(600),S(30),TOTAL(20),AVER(20),SD(20),VMIN(20),VMAX(20)TALL 480
C                                                                    TALL 490
       NV = 20                                                       TALL 502
       NO = 30                                                       TALL 504
C          CLEAR OUTPUT VECTORS AND INITIALIZE VMIN,VMAX             TALL 500
C                                                                    TALL 510
       IER=0                                                         TALL 511
       DO 1 K=1,NV                                                   TALL 520
       TOTAL(K)=0.0                                                  TALL 530
       AVER(K) = 0.0                                                 TALL 540
       SD(K) = 0.0                                                   TALL 550
       VMIN(K)=1.0E10                                                TALL 560
     1 VMAX(K)=-1.0E10                                               TALL 570
C                                                                    TALL 580
C          TEST SUBSET VECTOR                                        TALL 590
C                                                                    TALL 600
       SCNT=0.0                                                      TALL 610
       DO 7 J=1,NO                                                   TALL 620
       IJ=J-NO                                                       TALL 630
       IF(S(J)) 2,7,2                                                TALL 640
     2 SCNT=SCNT+1.0                                                 TALL 650
C                                                                    TALL 660
C          CALCULATE TOTAL, MINIMA, MAXIMA                           TALL 670
C                                                                    TALL 680
       DO 6 I=1,NV                                                   TALL 690
       IJ=IJ+NO                                                      TALL 700
       TOTAL(I)=TOTAL(I)+A(IJ)                                       TALL 710
       IF(A(IJ)-VMIN(I)) 3,4,4                                       TALL 720
     3 VMIN(I)=A(IJ)                                                 TALL 730
     4 IF(A(IJ)-VMAX(I)) 6,6,5                                       TALL 740
     5 VMAX(I)=A(IJ)                                                 TALL 750
     6 SD(I)=SD(I)+A(IJ)*A(IJ)                                       TALL 760
     7 CONTINUE                                                      TALL 770
C                                                                    TALL 780
C          CALCULATE MEANS AND STANDARD DEVIATIONS                   TALL 790
C                                                                    TALL 800
       IF (SCNT)8,8,9                                                TALL 801
     8 IER=1                                                         TALL 802
       GO TO 15                                                      TALL 803
     9 DO 10 I=1,NV                                                  TALL 810
    10 AVER(I)=TOTAL(I)/SCNT                                         TALL 820
       IF (SCNT-1.0) 13,11,13                                        TALL 821
    11 IER=2                                                         TALL 822
       DO 12 I=1,NV                                                  TALL 823
    12 SD(I)=0.0                                                     TALL 824
       GO TO 15                                                      TALL 825
    13 DO 14 I=1,NV                                                  TALL 826
    14 SD(I)=SQRT(ABS((SD(I)-TOTAL(I)*TOTAL(I)/SCNT)/(SCNT-1.0)))    TALL 830
    15 CALL EXIT                                                     TALL 840
       END                                                          TALL 850
```

Handwritten annotations:
- INTERCHANGED (560-570) (next to lines 560 and 570)
- DO 6 I=1,NO (next to line 690)
- PARENTHESIS CHANGE /SCNT)/SCNT-1.0)) (next to lines 824-830)

Fig 5. Source: Gould/Drongowski: A Controlled Psychological Study of
Computer Program Debugging. Oct 1972. IBM RC 4083. 39 pages.

	GROUP HINT	WRONG GUESSES PER LISTING	AVERAGE TIME TO FIND BUG (min.)	BUGS NOT FOUND IN A LISTING
"FIND THE BUG"	NO AID	.1 → 1.5	5.4 → 10.6	0–2
"IT IS "IF"	CLASS OF BUG	.1 → .8	1.2 → 9.6	0–2
TEST DATA	I/O	.2 → .9	6.3 → 16.9	1–2
+ CORRECT DATA	I/O + correct	.1 → .8	3.7 → 14.7	0–2
"BUG IN LINE 690"	LINE NUMBER	.1 → .7	1.9 → 3.5	0–1

Fig 6. Measures of program maintenance ease under different program documentation conditions: a bebugging example using 5 groups of 6 programmers (Gould/Drongowski, IBM RC 4083).

- group 1 had simply a source program listing (with comments)

- group 2 was told the class of bug ("a parenthesis error")

- group 3 was given some input data and its resulting output

- group 4 was given the same test data plus "correct" output

- group 5 was told the exact line number in the source program where the error could be corrected.

An analysis of the results indicates some very interesting possibilities:

1. The use of test data seems to be less effective than simple source program reading.

2. Bugs are more difficult for experienced programmers to find correctly in small well-defined modules than most of us would expect. No group avoided wrong guesses and in all the groups there were individuals who gave up the attempt to find bugs which they knew were present.

3. Variations between individuals in homogeneously selected groups of programmers are at least 2 to 1, and up to 10 to 1, which indicates the extreme caution necessary when interpreting measures based on individual performance.

The objective of this particular research was to determine which types of software improvements would most effectively contribute to programmer bug-finding ability.

Predicting degree of software project completion using bebugging method

When is a software project finally finished? I am not thinking of when it is planned to be finished or when it actually is finished, but of when it is finished according to the quality specifications which were (hopefully) laid down before the project was initiated.

How can we determine whether the program is really "halfway finished" or 99% ready, as the programmer says? And how can we predict the remaining effort necessary to complete a program when we are in the middle of the project and unexpected delays and difficulties have occurred?

I believe (but I should warn the reader that I have at present no experience on this point) that we can use an adaptation of the bebugging method as a practical measuring tool.

The method is well known to zoologists, who use it to estimate the number of fish in a pond or a butterfly population.

How many fish <u>are</u> there in a pond or a lake? Let's say that a reasonably large sample of 1000 fish are marked and then allowed to mix for a while with the total population of the pond. If we then take a new sample of 1000 fish and find that 50 of these have our markings on them, this gives us 20,000 fish as a reasonable estimate if we accept that the original sample was random and representative and that the remixing of the fish was homogeneous.

Estimating the number of bugs of particular types that are left in a program

Before we can estimate the remaining completion time for a program, we first have to find out what percentage of the bugs that we intend to remove have actually been removed. This, of course, is quite interesting in itself, since the percentage of bugs removed is somehow related to the operational failure rate (or reliability function) of the program.

Let us insert, for the sake of simplicity, 100 bugs (see discussion of

Fagan's Inspection Statistics below to find out exactly what kind of bugs to insert) in a representative sample.

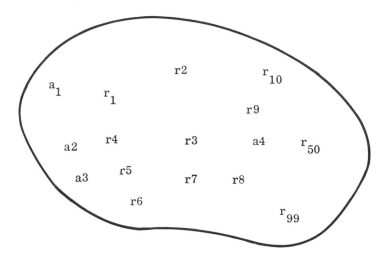

Fig 7. Artificially inserted bugs (a) mixed with real bugs (r) in a
    program. The artificial bugs are known and controlled, and can
    be removed at will. They serve to "calibrate" the process of
    finding real bugs. If the type and number of artificial bugs found
    are related to the real bugs found during the same period
    estimates of the type and quantity of remaining bugs can be made,
    and this gives us a measure of the progress towards the specified
    program reliability.

If at a particular point in the debugging we record a collection of 550
bugs found, of which 50 are artificially inserted and 500 are real, this
gives an estimate of about 500 real bugs left of the type corresponding
to the type of artificial bug inserted.

There may, of course be far more real bugs, but these would be of a
different type for which no corresponding artificial bugs have been inserted.

Debugging curves

If step-by-step experience of the rate of bug detection is collected
during program testing, experience curves similar to the ones in Fig
8 can be drawn.

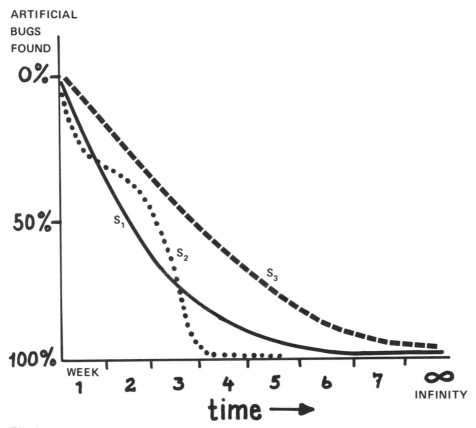

Fig 8.

Diminishing returns on debugging effort

In real and large systems one would expect to find that there is a point of diminishing returns (in bugs found) on investment (of program debugging effort). Getting absolutely all the bugs out of a real program is now recognized as a task requiring an almost limitless amount of effort.

This is not the place to explain why, but this assertion is supported by the fact that in 1972, in the 20th major version of their approximately 3 million statement "360 Operating System", IBM officially reported approximately 12, 000 distinct new bugs in the system. At least 1, 000 bugs had been discovered in each of the 20 "releases" in spite of 24-hour usage of the program for several years by thousands of computer installations. Small programs are no different, as shown by the results of Gould's bebugging experiment with small subroutines.

Now this "law of diminishing bug-find rate" will probably motivate you to specify that the program is considered "complete" when, say, 95% of the bugs (as measured by means of the artificial bugs) have been removed. The 96th percentage might indeed double the total debugging effort. But how can we know? Well, we can't know in advance without the benefit of previous experience. This is why it is important to draw debugging experience curves, which serve thereafter as guides to the degree to which we should debug. The cost of debugging is roughly proportionate to the time used.

Now, one reason for stopping debugging is because of the extra cost or time involved. It is, however, necessary to keep on debugging until a satisfactory level of reliability is achieved.

How can we possibly know how reliable a program will be before it is run operationally?

We can't know anything for sure, but we should be able to make reasonable enough estimates to give us practical control tools for measuring program cost and quality. The problem here will simply be one of the cost versus the value of additional accuracy.

Estimating program reliability and cost of development

Let us assume that a large number of programs are debugged to the 95% level (5% of the bugs are left), using a consistent method for artificial bug setting and evaluation.

If the mean time to discovery of additional bugs is calculated, we would then be able to draw experience curves for the mean time to bug discovery for programs with 95% debuggedness. Similarly we could produce corresponding curves for any degree of debuggedness (96%, 96.5%, 96.6%, etc.), which would aid program designers in making decisions as to the necessary degree of debuggedness for a satisfactory reliability, at an acceptable price (using the debugging experience curves table to estimate costs).

Estimating remaining project effort

When the degree of debuggedness which must be achieved is established, then, during the project, debugging experience curves should make it possible to give reasonably accurate estimates as to the remaining effort required to reach the specified goal for debuggedness.

For example, you may write a program which is characteristic of the "S2" (see debugging experience curves above) class of programs. Your specified quality goal may be 90% and you have already found 50% of the artificial bugs in 2 months of effort. How long will it be before you get to the 90% mark? Using a ruler, you can find out that about 40% more effort is needed and the estimated time of completion can be replanned for 3 1/2 weeks from now. This won't necessarily turn out to be true, but it may be the best planning tool available. You may even want to change the prediction by reallocation of testing resources and people.

PROBABILITY OF BUG DETECTION DURING OPERATION (FAILURE PROBABILITY)

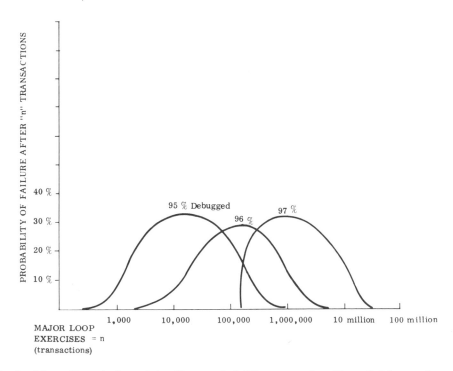

Fig 9. Mean time to bug detection probability, as a function of debuggedness degree measured by means of artificial bug calibration. Hypothetical values. Real values must be developed for each environment.

35

Bebugging method used to study bug finding rate and desk debugging effectiveness

A software certification project sponsored by Bell Labs and conducted by IBM Systems Assurance Department of the Federal Systems Division ("Safeguard") in 1971, included an experiment in code reading. The raw data from this experiment were used by Jelinski and Moranda of McDonnell Douglas (JELINSKI-IEEE-73) to analyze the effectiveness of program source code reading as a means of debugging (as opposed to the use of software tools for debugging). The conclusion they arrived at was that "the process of desk-checking becomes expensive, and some combination of desk-checking and machine assisted debugging would seem to be optimal".

The conclusion seems rather broad when one sees the limited number of factors that were studied, but the experiment does serve to illustrate an actual example of the use of bebugging (or seeding of errors). Two different sets of assumptions were made concerning the rate of finding the remaining bugs at any point in the process. The details of the reasoning used by the authors are not included here. The following remarks from the paper may provide insight into the bebugging method.

"4 errors per 100 instructions was used as the seeding rate" on the average.

The time estimates for finding remaining bugs refer only to the artificial bugs. There is no implication of ability to determine that a program really is 100% bug-free. However, it is amusing to note that "there were many indigenous (or unseeded) errors which were found along with the seeded errors ... it had been assumed by the designers of the code reading experiment that the programs were perfectly clean at the time of seeding."

The reader is referred to Fig 10 for the results presented in this paper.

Making artificial bugs representative

All bugs are not created equal.

Obviously we can get more information about the kind of bugs we are finding and, in particular, the kind we are not currently finding, if the bugs we insert are somehow representative of the bugs we should be finding.

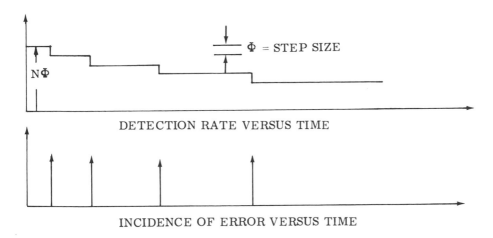

DETECTION RATE VERSUS TIME

INCIDENCE OF ERROR VERSUS TIME

Fig 10. 1 Bebugging used to estimate the source program reading time to find all bugs (performed by IBM in Safeguard Code Certification Experiment, for Bell Labs, 1971). Source: JELINSKI-IEEE-73

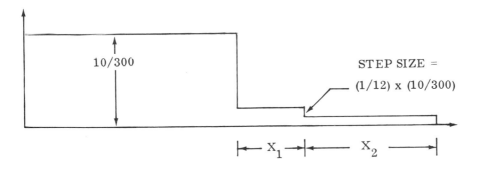

Fig 10. 2 Model for second method of estimation

How then do we make a representative collection of bugs we should be finding for a program whose bugs are as yet unknown?

Well, we can start by borrowing a few principles from Gallup opinion polls. The representative samples must be based on a proportional representation of the total population of errors. How do we know? By collecting error statistics by error type as a part of the inspection process (FAGAN-IBM-21572 and later).

Another approach would be to assume that bugs can be caused by any

Fig 10.3
Estimates of Additional Reading Time
(Method I)

Reader#	First Reading Time . (Min.)	Errors Present	Errors Found	Est. Addit. Time	Standard Deviation of – Estimate
#1	477.8	29	21	1044	475
#2	543.9	29	21	1188	540
#3	300.0	12	10	281	210
#4	375.0	12	11	178	178
#5	360.0	12	10	252	252

Fig 10.4
Estimates of Additional Reading Time
(Method II)

Reader#	First Reading Time (Min.)	Errors Present	Errors Found	Est Addit. Time	Standard Deviation of Estimate
#1	477.8	29	21	1793	815
#2	543 9	29	21	2040	928
#3	300.0	12	10	540	403
#4	375.0	12	11	409	409
#5	360.0	12	10	648	484

one particular type of programming statement, and insert artificial bugs in proportion to the frequency of occurrence of that type of statement.

As an example of such a census see the statistics for FORTRAN and APL presented in Fig 11.

This method ensures that we insert bugs in reasonable proportion to the statement type, and that each statement type is included.

Relationship of program statement type frequency to error frequency per type

Fig 12 (NAGY-IBM-3407, an interesting example of software metrics studied by means of automatic collection of program change data) shows that the assumption that bugs are spread evenly by statement type is only very roughly true. The number of changes in Nagy's experiments are presumably bug corrections, and there are certain types which predominate according to the (log. !) scale in the illustration.

Consequently, we should try to base our artificial bug insertion on relevant bug statistics if at all possible.

Estimating the probability distribution of remaining software errors by bebugging

M. Lipow of TRW Systems Group has done an analysis of the bebugging method entitled "Estimation of Software Package Residual Errors" (LIPOW-TRW-72-09).

He bases his initial study on two assumptions which are convenient simplifications:

1. The probability of finding an error is constant, independent of the number of errors previously found.

2. At most one error can be found during one trial (or test case).

While referring the reader to his paper for the detailed reasoning, I should like to show some of the tables he has worked out, in order that the reader may get some additional insight into, and perhaps useful tools from the possibilities offered by the bebugging method.

STATEMENT POPULATION COUNTS = REPRESENTATIVE SAMPLES

Statement	Number of occurences	Percentage
INTEGER	74	4.6
DIMENSION	38	2.4
COMMON	89	5.5
DATA	2	.1
GOTO	117	7.3
IF	262	16.4
DO	68	4.3
CONTINUE	54	3.4
RETURN	31	1.9
END	31	1.9
FORMAT	6	.35
READ	4	.25
WRITE	4	.25
ASSIGN(=)	643	40.
CALL	177	11.
LABELS	568	35
DUMMY VARIABLES	287	
COMMON VARIABLES	40	

Total number of statements : 1600

APL VERSION

Operator	Number of occurences	Percentage
←	214	20.4
.	156	14.9
/	118	11.3
→	114	10.9
=	69	6.6
:	69	6.6
ρ	65	6.2
+	36	3.4
≠	34	3.2
∇	34	3.2
∊	32	3.
∨	29	2.8
∼	19	1.8
-	18	1.7
∧	13	1.2
ι	11	1.
<	5	.5
>	4	.4
×	3	.3
≥	2	.2

The other *APL* operators do not appear in this example.

Fig 11. Source: APL Congress 73 Copenhagen Proceedings "APL in a
Two-Step Programming Technique..."

NUMBER OF STATEMENTS (COMPILED PROGRAMS ONLY)

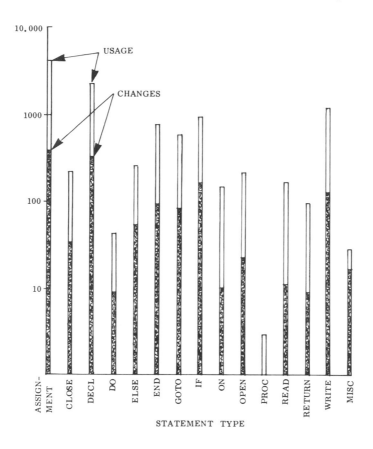

Fig 12. Distribution of usage and changes according to statement type.

Fig 13 gives a rough idea of the range of total bugs which might be left in the program. See next page.

For example if we seeded 100 artificial bugs into a program and tested until we had observed 50 errors (real + seeded) altogether, 25 of which were seeded and 25 of which were real, then we can estimate the total number of errors before testing to have been:

$$= \frac{25 \text{ (real errors found)}}{25 \text{ (seeded found)}} \times 50 \text{ (originally seeded)}$$

$$= 50$$

A rough guess at the remaining number of errors is: <u>50</u> (our rough estimate of the total of original real errors) <u>minus</u> 25 (the number of real errors found thus far) <u>which is</u> 25 (estimated remaining errors).

Looking at Lipow's Table 2 (on the line "see Tab. 3"), we find that this set of values allows us to get an impression of how much we can trust our estimate. The square root of the mean square deviation (RMSD) is 12.72, which for most practical purposes can be read as ±13. If somebody were to ask us for an estimate of the remaining bugs we could say "about 50". If they pressed us about the reliability of our estimate we could say that it was accurate "give or take a dozen". If they really want a better estimate we could look at Lipow's Table 3, Fig 14, and tell them that there is a "worst case" possibility of about 138 more errors.

Perhaps the programming manager is not satisfied with such rough guesses. A look at Fig 15 gives us a hint as to how we can improve the guess. Looking at the next line of Fig 13 (marked "see Tab 3. ") we see that the more errors we observe (in this case 100 instead of just 50) before making our estimate as to the remaining errors, the more confidence we can have in our estimate of 50 remaining errors.

The ± estimate in the right-hand column of the "see Tab 4" line in Fig 13 is 6.23, and looking at the corresponding detailed table (Fig 15) we can make observations like:

- At worst there could be as many as 81 bugs.

- There are almost certainly at least 26 bugs left,

- but it is 99% certain that we have no more than 63 bugs left.

If you are armed with historical data about the cost of finding and repairing software bugs (see Fagan below for examples), and you "know" that each bug costs for example a programmer hour, then you have a reasonably good basis for estimating probable completion dates, the amount of computer testing time needed, and the amount of additional manpower resources needed in order to complete the testing on the agreed schedule.

Fig 13 is not of course intended to be a complete table for real life use in bebugging. The values can be calculated by standard statistical programs. The real purpose is to illustrate the effect of a larger "errors found" ("r") sample on our ability to predict with greater accuracy the number of errors left in the program. Take a look at the last three lines on the table, for example, and notice how the increasing size of the sample (50, 100, 200) reduces the errors-remaining deviation estimate

TABLE 2.

CONDITIONAL MEAN AND ROOT MEAN SQUARE DEVIATION OF ESTI-
MATOR OF NUMBER OF INDIGENOUS SOFTWARE ERRORS AS A FUNC-
TION OF ACTUAL NUMBER OF INDIGENOUS ERRORS AND NUMBER OF
SEEDED ERRORS, GIVEN THE TOTAL NUMBER OF ERRORS OBSERVED

Actual Number of Errors		Observed Total Errors	Mean	RMSD
n_I	$n_S n_S$	r	$E(n_I \mid r)$	$\sigma(\hat{n}_I \mid r)$
10	10	5	13.82	12.57
10	10	10	11.06	6.22
10	20	10	10.90	6.77
10	20	20	9.70	2.91
10	30	10	10.70	7.59
10	30	30	9.57	1.99
10	50	10	10.71	8.93
10	50	50	9.42	1.44
20	20	10	23.99	17.90
20	20	20	20.86	7.26
50	50	10	62.94	53.08
50	50	50	50.74	10.46
50	100	20	52.99	24.95
50	100 see Tab. 3	50	50.59	12.72
50	100 see Tab. 4	100	49.71	6.23
100	200	50	102.19	28.59
100	200	100	100.48	12.34
100	200	200	99.77	8.78

Est. Tot Bugs in All *	Total Number of Bugs Put in	Number of Real and Artificial Bugs Found Thus Far in the Tests	"± Estimate"

$$* \ n_I = \frac{\text{no. real errors found}}{\text{no. seeded errors found}} \times \text{total no. seeded errors}$$

Fig 13. Source: M. Lipow, TRW-SS-72-09.

TABLE 3

NO. OF UNKNOWN ERRORS= 50 (calculated estimate of n_I, see previous table)
NO. OF SEEDED ERRORS= 100
NO. OF TRIALS FINDING ERRORS= 50 (real plus artificial bugs found altogether)

MEAN	BIAS	RMS
50.59	.59	12.72

$(= MEAN - n_1)$

DISTRIBUTION OF MAX. LIKELIHOOD ESTIMATOR OF NO. OF UNKNOWN ERRORS:

ESTIMATOR	PROBABILITY	CUM. PROB.
11	.00001	.00001
13	.00004	.00005
16	.00019	.00024
19	.00075	.00099
21	.00250	.00349
25	.00702	.01051
28	.01673	.02724
31	.03420	.06143
35	06029	.12173
38	.09212	.21385
42	.12245	.33630
47	.14205	.47835
51	.14417	.62252
56	.12827	.75079 (75 % chance that not more
61	.10019	.85098 than 56 errors remain)
66	.06877	.91975
72	.04151	.96126
78	.02204	.98331
85	.01029	.99360
92	.00422	.99782
100	.00152	.99934
108	.00048	.99983
117	.00013	.99996
127	.00003	.99999
138	.00001	1.00000
150	.00000	1.00000

THIS IS A LIST OF A   THIS IS THE PROBABILITY
POSSIBLE NUMBER OF   THAT THAT NUMBER OF BUGS
BUGS WHICH REALLY   REMAIN
REMAIN

Fig 14.

TABLE 4

NO. OF UNKNOWN ERRORS= 50
NO. OF SEEDED ERRORS= 100
NO. OF TRIALS FINDING ERRORS= 100

MEAN	BIAS	RMS
49.71	-.29	6.23

DISTRIBUTION OF MAX. LIKELIHOOD ESTIMATOR OF NO. OF UNKNOWN ERRORS:

ESTIMATOR	PROBABILITY	CUM. PROB.
26	.00001	.00001
28	.00003	.00004
29	.00013	.00017
31	.00048	.00066
33	.00152	.00218
35	.00422	.00640
36	.01029	.01669
38	.02204	.03874
40	.04151	.08025
42	.06877	.14902
44	.10019	.24921
47	.12827	.37748
49	.14417	.52165
51	.14205	.66370
53	.12245	.78615
56	.09212	.87827
58	.06029	.93857
61	.03420	.97276
63	.01673	.98949
66	.00702	.99651
69	.00250	.99901
72	.00075	.99976
75	.00019	.99995
78	.00004	.99999
81	.00001	1.00000

Fig 15.

(± 28.59, ± 12.34, ± 8.78). These three phases may be thought of as being three different points in time during a project. In simple terms, the further along in our debugging effort we are, the greater is our ability to estimate the remaining work.

By observation, the accuracy of the estimate improves as the number of seeded bugs added increases, as long as a correspondingly large number of errors is found compared to the total of seeded plus artificial errors.

The "mean" number, of course, allows us to calculate the statistical bias (Mean $- n_1$) that is needed to calculate the probability that a particular number of errors is the correct one, and it serves as an indicator of error.

Relationship between artificial bugs, test cases run, and software reliability

Girard and Rault of Thomson-CSF of France have provided a number of useful insights into the uses of bebugging (GIRARD-73). It is worth noting that they mention that their ideas are a technology transfer from techniques which they have developed or applied in their electrical engineering work on logical circuits. This is not unexpected, since hardware is really just a hard form of software. In other words, software metrics theory and applications can expect to derive much inspiration and guidance from known hardware engineering techniques, as will be obvious in the rest of this text.

Fig 16, taken from their paper, provides some insight into the role of artificial bugs in calculating the program reliability metric (which in this case is expressed indirectly as percentage of remaining bugs cleaned out as each test case is run).

The table (Fig 16) is developed on the basis of some simplifications which the authors argue are reasonable and necessary. In this particular case the authors make use of dual independent versions of the program (one in APL and one in FORTRAN) as a comparison device for detecting the artificial bugs, which are inserted only in the FORTRAN program. All test cases are given as input to both versions of the algorithm, and any test case which demonstrates the presence of an artificial bug is detected by means of the unequal output which the APL version will produce. (The dual code will be discussed later.)

Test cases are generated by random selection from all possible test cases.

A TABLE WHICH ALLOWS AN ESTIMATE OF THE TOTAL MINIMUM
NUMBER OF TEST CASES WHICH MUST BE RUN TO REMOVE ARTIFICIAL
BUGS WHEN TEST CASE GENERATION IS BY SIMULATION

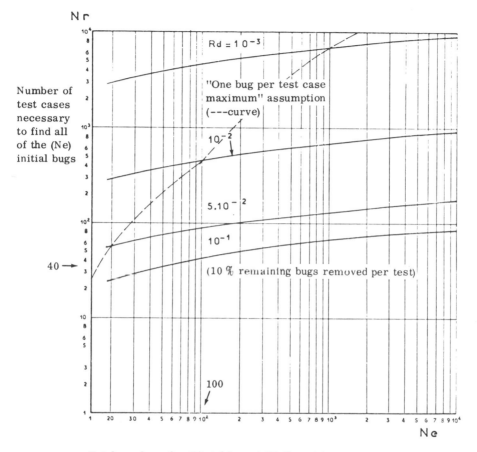

Total number of artificial bugs initially put in program

N_r as a function of N_e and R_d

Fig 16. Example: R_d is the detecting power of each test case, the percentage of the <u>rest</u> of the original set of bugs it will remove with
each new test case. $R_d = 10^{-1}$ for 100 initial bugs requires at
least 40 test cases to detect all the bugs. The bugs diminish with
each test case like the series 100, 90, 81, 72, 65, 59, 53 ...,
and it takes 40 such test cases to reach down to about 1 remaining
bug.
Source: GIRARD-73, Modification and interpretation suggested by
Rault to Gilb 750909.

It is interesting to note that both test case generation and error detection are capable of complete automation, although this is no requirement.

An important assumption and simplification is that the dual code is constructed so logically independently that faults in one program do not occur at identical points in the other version.

Girard and Rault remark that bebugging can be used to "assess the 'detecting power' of test cases generated randomly" (GIRARD-73). We can find out how few randomly-generated test cases, from a given set of possible test cases, are necessary for finding a certain percentage of the artificial bugs.

Automation of the bebugging measurement tool

Certain aspects of the bebugging method are programmable, although, to my knowledge, this has yet not been done. Having automatic bebugging programs available would seem to considerably ease the burden of using the method and would lead to wider use.

Here is a list of the jobs which a "bebugging program" could be expected to do:

- bug insertion

- recording of the original state of the source program

- restoring the program to its original state (before bebugging)

- determining the number of bugs to insert (based on program size and the accuracy required in the measure)

- determining the type of bug to insert (based on statistics of type of bug found, which could be gathered automatically)

- evaluation of whether artificial bugs had been corrected (this would give a rough, but automatic estimate; another approach (suggested in GIRARD-73) is automatic detection of whether the bug has been exercised by means of comparison of outputs of dual independent program versions, where only one version is bebugged)

- statistical reporting on bug-finding rate and type of bug

- estimation of confidence in the program reliability

- estimation of mean time to failure of the program

- estimation of the number of test cases which must be run.

All of these tasks seem simple to do, at least if done roughly, although most of them seem capable of endless sophistication.

```
┌─────────────────────────┐
│  BEBUGGING SOFTWARE     │                    CAN
└─────────────────────────┘
                                        JUST LIKE HUMAN
• DELETE LINES                          BEBUGGERS
            IF   A = B
              OR C > D ⟩→
                THEN
                    DO


• DOUBLE LINES
            C = D
            A = A + 1
            A = A + 1


• REVERSE LINES
            A = C
            IF   A > B   THEN . . . .


• CHANGE CHARACTERS
            I̶F̶ ̶A̶ ̶=̶ ̶>̶B̶ ← IF A > B


• CHANGE CONTROL CARDS
            //A  DD   BLOCKSIZE = 100⟋out
```

Fig 17.

49

Inspection of the software development process

Software component inspection as a metric instrument

Software development may be viewed as a continuous process in which the following types of change take place:

- refinement of specifications through several levels of rough specification, to more detailed and precise specifications

- corrections (additions, replacements or deletions) to the software when errors (in relation to higher-level specifications) are detected.

Furthermore, the development process may be viewed as a process which is striving towards a set of arbitrarily defined functional, quality and resource usage goals. The process can be compared to a ship navigating at sea (an exercise left to the reader's imagination).

Just as the ship's captain needs a variety of instruments, such as maps of different scales, lookouts, different radar and navigation instruments, fuel consumption meters, and Veritas inspections of seaworthness at periodic intervals, the captains of the software ships will be more likely to succeed in meeting their specifications if the instruments for measuring the development process are sufficiently detailed and accurate, and used at a sufficiently early point in the work process.

"Inspection" as practiced at IBM Systems Communications Division

Michael E. Fagan (FAGAN-IBM-21572) and his colleague Rodney R. Larson (LARSON-IBM-21586) have developed some simple but powerful methods for measuring the quality of the software development process.

They have applied their ideas on a realistically large scale and carefully verified the productivity and reliability increases which can mainly, it seems, be attributed to management making use of the software metrics.

An overall view of the inspection process, as it is currently (mid-1975) applied, is described in the following illustration (Fig 18).

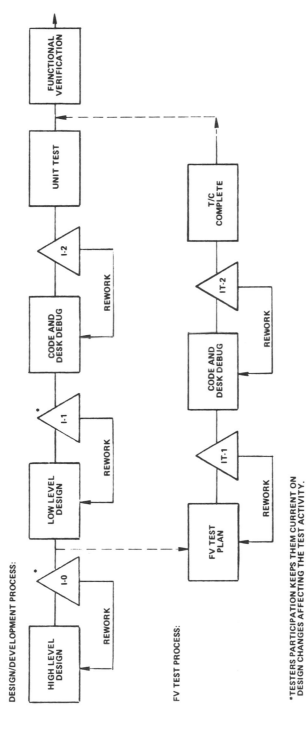

INSPECTION PROCESS FLOW

DESIGN/DEVELOPMENT PROCESS:

FV TEST PROCESS:

*TESTERS PARTICIPATION KEEPS THEM CURRENT ON
DESIGN CHANGES AFFECTING THE TEST ACTIVITY.

Fig 18. Source: R. Larson, "Test plan and test case inspection specification", IBM TR 21.586.

51

Inspection process flow

Inspection is essentially an "audit" or quality assurance. The major
objective of inspection is to "find errors and omissions". The inspection
process consists of five major phases (from "Planning" to "Followup",
as can be seen in Fig 19), each of which has its own separate objective.

In quantitative terms the inspection is carried out (after individual pre-
paratory reading of documentation) by about four trained inspectors
at a two-hour meeting.

Inspections have been applied in practice to the logicware (I-0, I-1 and
I-2) and to the testware (IT-1 and IT-2) at the points in the process
illustrated in Fig 18.

There are plans to apply the inspection procedure to:

- interconnection inspections ("IF")

- inspection of fixes and changes

- inspection of publications (documentation).

The observant reader will have noticed that there is no inspection of the
logicware after it has been compiled and run ("I-3"). The reason is that
Fagan measured a net loss of programmer productivity (benefit of I-3
minus its cost) of 20 programmer hours per thousand lines (not comments)
of code produced, when the early inspections (I-1 and I-2) were carried
out.

The functional verification of the compiled programs is carried out by
means of the test cases, which are themselves subject to inspections
(IT-1 and IT-2).

Data collection of the error metrics

The key to the inspection measuring tool is the Design Inspection Report
(Fig 20). The illustration is a design inspection report used by Fagan of
IBM to collect summaries of errors found in the inspection of the low-
level logicware design. This is, effectively, reading of pseudocode,
which is approximately one-tenth of the detail volume of the program
coding inspected in the next phase.

In terms of Girard and Rault's use of dual code (GIRARD-73 and DEMARS-

INSPECTION PROCEDURE

Operation	Description	Objectives	Comments
1. PLANNING	Establishing the schedules, designating the participants, and requesting the inspection material	To ensure that schedules and participants are established and materials available	Occurs before inspection material is available
2. PREPARATION	Participants use distributed material to prepare for the inspection	Allows participants to come to the inspection prepared to find errors	Occurs after material distributed and before the inspection
3. INSPECTION	Formal process of inspecting the distributed material	To find errors and omissions	A meeting led by the Moderator held after preparation by all participants is complete.
4. REWORK	The process of fixing those problems identified at the inspection	Provides time for identified problems to be corrected	Moderator determines necessity of reinspection based on number and magnitude of problems
5. FOLLOW-UP	The process of accountability of problem resolution	To ensure all problems are satisfactorily resolved	Exit criteria requires all problems resolved. Data from inspection included in data base

Fig 19. Source: Larson, IBM TR 21.586.

73) this would correspond to an inspection of the APL logicware (which also takes about one-tenth of the effort of the corresponding FORTRAN program according to the above references).

The inspection report is tailored to:

- the level and type of inspection

- the programming language or documentation standard used

- the management's belief in what categories of error it is important to exercise control over.

The errors found are logged in detail elsewhere, and are summarized in the Design Inspection Report according to:

- type of problem

- missing, wrongly implemented, extra (all with reference to the previous level of specifications or to installation standards)

- seriousness (1, 2, 3, 4). This is used to weight the estimates of "rework hours" according to previous experience of repair of the type and degree of the fault.

All this data is collected in a project manager data base and serves as a management information system for scheduling, for indicating the need to initiate changes (retraining, new aids, reorganization), and as a tool for measuring the effect of changes ("Did the change really solve the problem?").

Examples of the kind of report which can be generated from this data base are shown in Figs. 20-22. Fagan stresses the importance of management concentration on the statistically dominating problem areas (indicated by the arrows on the left of the illustrations). Otherwise, he points out (personal communication), there is a strong tendency to get involved in panic reactions to single errors, which are less productive than management action on the most frequently occurring problems.

Identifying error-prone logicware modules by the inspection process

Fig 23 is another example of a useful report from this data collection. The data shown is from the six worst modules of a group of real software modules (whose names have been altered).

DESIGN INSPECTION REPORT

— Follow Up Sheet —

I. (1) MODULE/MACRO NAME _____ (2) COMPONENT _____ (3) FUNCTION _____
(4) DESIGNER _____ (5) CHART DATE _____
(6) DEVELOPER _____ (7) RELEASE NUMBER _____ (8) INCREMENT NO. _____
(9) TESTER _____ (10) MODERATOR _____
(11) ESTIMATED LINES OF CODE (NEW, CHANGED OR DELETED) _____

(12) SYSTEM: ☐ ☐ ☐ ☐

OTHER ☐ ☐

☐

II. (13) VALID PROBLEMS

	Missing				Wrong				Extra				Sub-Total	
	1	2	3	4	1	2	3	4	1	2	3	4		
													LO	
													TB	
													IC	
													CB	
													CU	
													RM	
													RU	
													MA	
													IR	
													PD	
													MD	
													ST	
													PR	
													L3	
													FS	
													MN	
													PE	
													OT	
														100

1. Logic (LO)
2. Tests and Branches (TB)
3. Interface Calls (IC)
4. CB Definition (CD)
5. CB Usage (CU)
6. Return Codes/Messages (RM)
7. Register Usage (RU)
8. Module Attributes (MA)
9. Interface Requirements (IR)
10. Passed Data Areas (PD)
11. More Detail (MD)
12. Standards (ST)
13. Prologue or Prose (PR)
14. Higher Level Design Documen. (L3)
15. FPFS (FS)
16. Maintainability (MN)
17. Performance (PE)
18. Other (OT)

III. (17) ACTUAL MAN HOURS OF INSPECTION _____
(18) ESTIMATED REWORK HOURS _____
(19) ESTIMATED LINES OF CODE IN REWORK _____

Fig 20. Source: Fagan, IBM TR 21.572.

55

INSPECTION FILE

Summary of CODE Inspections by Error Type

		Missing	Wrong	Extra	Errors	Error %
VP	Individual Name					
CC	Code Comments	5	17	1	23	6.6
CU	CB Usage	3	21	1	25	7.2
DE	Design Error	31	32	14	77	22.1 ←
F1			8		8	2.3
IR	Interconnect Calls	7	9	3	19	5.5
LO	Logic	33	49	10	92	26.4 ←
MN	Maintainability	5	7	2	14	4.0
OT	Other					
PE	Performance	3	2	5	10	2.9
PR	Prologue/Prose	25	24	3	52	14.9 ←
PU	PL/S or Bal Use	4	9	1	14	4.0
RU	Register Usage	4	2		6	1.7
SU	Storage Usage	1			1	.3
TB	Test & Branch	2	5		7	2.0
		123	185	40	348	100.0

Fig 21.

Experience has shown that modules which have a higher number of errors reported per thousand object code locations will later prove to give rise to a disproportionate amount of work (testing, maintenance, etc.). It pays off to identify such modules early with a view to taking some major corrective action (before the problems start occurring), such as a total rewrite of the module.

Weinberg has told me that he had also observed that a very small part of the logicware was the cause of most of the maintenance effort. Consequently, he said one installation allowed the maintenance programmers to use a small percentage of their time to select and rewrite those modules which gave the most problems (according to their experience). In a surprisingly short time, he reported, the error rates and maintenance effort were substantially reduced. Obviously, systematically collected error metrics would serve as good evidence for initiating a rewrite of particularly troublesome parts of a system.

Fagan also observes that error-proneness may result in "harder" testing, reinspection, or redesign, as well as recoding.

INSPECTION FILE
Summary of DESIGN Inspections by Error Type

VP	Individual Name	Missing	Wrong	Extra	Errors	Error%	
CD	CB Definition	16	2		18	3.5	} 10.4
CU	CB Usage	18	17	1	36	6.9	
FS	FPFS	1			1	.2	
IC	Interconnect Calls	18	9		27	5.2	
IR	Interconnect Reqts	4	5	2	11	2.1	
LO	Logic	126	57	24	207	39.8 ←	
L3	Higher Lvl Docu	1		1	2	.4	
MA	Mod Attributes	1			1	.2	
MD	More Detail	24	6	2	32	6.2	
MN	Maintainability	8	5	3	16	3.1	
OT	Other	15	10	10	35	6.7	
PD	Pass Data Areas		1		1	.2	
PE	Performance	1	2	3	6	1.2	
PR	Prologue/Prose	44	38	7	89	17.1 ←	
RM	Return Code/Msg	5	7	2	14	2.7	
RU	Register Usage	1	2		3	.6	
ST	Standards						
TB	Test & Branch	12	7	2	21	4.0	
		295	168	57	520	100.0	
		57 %	32%	11%			

Fig 22.

MOST ERROR-PRONE MODULES BASED ON I_1 AND I_2
(Example)

Module Name	No. Errors	Lines of Code	Error Density (Errors/K.Loc)	
Echo	4	128	31	
Zulu	10	323	31	
Foxtrot	3	107	28	
Alpha	7	264	27	
Lima	2	106	19	← Average
Delta	3	195	15	Error Rate
⋮	⋮	⋮	⋮	
	67	⋮		

Fig 23. Source: Fagan, IBM TR 21.572

Analysis of error type frequency against expected values

Fagan points out, using the illustration "Distribution of Error Types" (Fig 24), that the analysis of large and statistically improbable deviations of particular error types, from the historically normal distribution of that error type, can allow the manager to fix the problem, providing such an analysis is carried out on an early ("first 5% of production") sample of the software being produced. In the example given, the internal interconnections seem like a candidate for analysis and possible correction.

DISTRIBUTION OF ERROR TYPES

(Example)

	No. Errors	%	Normal/Usual Distribution %
Logic	23	35	44
Interconnection (Internal)	21	31 ?	18
Control Blocks	6	9	13
–	.	8	10
–	.	7	7
–	.	6	6
–	.	4	2
		100%	100%

Fig 24. Source: Fagan IBM TR 21.572

Use of inspection metrics to design inspection checklists

The detailed lists of errors found during inspections are analyzed and from them lists of "typical error types to look for" are made.

Fagan reported to me that the use of checklists of the sort in Fig 25 improve the productivity of the inspection process to a significant extent.

"Numerous experiences have shown that people have to be taught or prompted to find errors effectively" (Fagan, TR 21.572 p.15). "So it is prudent to condition them to seek the high occurrence, high cost error types, and then describe the clues which usually betray the presence of each error type."

EXAMPLES OF WHAT TO EXAMINE WHEN LOOKING FOR ERRORS

I_1 Logic

Missing

1. Are All Constants Defined?
2. Are All Unique Values Explicitly Tested on Input Parameters?
3. Are Values Stored after They Are Calculated?
4. Are All Defaults Checked Explicitly Tested on Input Parameters?
5. If Character Strings Are Created Are They Complete, Are All Delimiters Shown?
6. If a Keyword Has Many Unique Values, Are They All Checked?
7. If a Queue Is Being Manipulated, Can the Execution Be Interrupted; If So, Is Queue Protected by a Locking Structure; Can Queue Be Destroyed Over an Interrupt?
8. Are Registers Being Restored on Exits?
9. Are Queuing/Dequeuing Should Any Value Be Decremented/Incremented?
10. Are All Keywords Tested in Macro?
11. Are All Keyword Related Parameters Tested in Service Routine?
12. Are Queues Being Held in Isolation So That Subsequent Interrupting Requestors Are Receiving Spurious Returns Regarding the Held Queue?
13. Should Any Registers Be Saved on Entry?
14. Are All Increment Counts Properly Initialized (0 or 1)?

Wrong

1. Are Absolutes Shown Where There Should Be Symbolics?
2. On Comparison of Two Bytes, Should All Bits Be Compared?
3. On Built Data Strings, Should They Be Character or Hex?
4. Are Internal Variables Unique or Confusing If Concatenated?

Extra

1. Are All Blocks Shown in Design Necessary or Are They Extraneous?

Fig 25. An example of IBM detailed design Inspection checklist for one single class of error ("Logic"). Source: Fagan IBM TR 21.572.

The use of inspection in application programs written in COBOL

One computer user developed the COBOL inspection checklist which the reader will find in Appendix A.

59

After two months' use of inspected code (I-1 and I-2) with one early applications program user of inspection, no errors were found.

Eighty percent of the total errors found before operation were found during one of the inspections. The remaining 20% were found during program testing.

The estimated productivity saving (compared to estimate based on history) was a net (after inspection costs) saving of 30%.

The results were evaluated as <u>not</u> being due to the Hawthorne effect, since the group measured was under constant study for productivity anyway.

Direct effort in use of inspection as a measurement tool

Fagan reports the rate experienced for the various parts of the inspection process, in Fig 27.

This is in units of non-commentary lines of source code of PLS (abbreviated as LOC in the figure). At a public presentation of the method (FTC-5, Paris, June 20, 1975) Fagan summarized this by saying that 1000 lines of code take 30 to 35 programmer hours to inspect.

However, even when the cost of measuring this is considered, he reports that Design Inspection (I-1) results in a net saving of 94 programmer hours per thousand lines of code. With Code Inspection (in both I-1 and I-2 he deducts the rework, or correction time, as well as inspection time) he reports savings of 51 programmer hours.

Error rework amounted to 78 programmer hours per thousand lines of source code for design inspection and 36 programmer hours for source code inspection rework.

His conclusion, even accounting for an insignificant 0.9% difference due to the Hawthorne Effect (better results when people know they are being studied) is that the net productivity increase due to his initial use of inspection metrics was a 23% productivity increase for the programmers. In addition, his inspected code had 38% fewer errors than code inspected by conventional review methods. Obviously, then, the <u>real</u> productivity of the method is far greater than 23% when we consider the effort needed to increase reliability by that much.

INSPECTION SPECIFICATION
Examples of What to Examine When Looking for Errors

I_2 Test Branch

Is Correct Condition Tested (If X = ON vs. If X = OFF)?

Is (Are) Correct Variable(s) Used for Test
(If X = ON vs. If Y = ON)?

Are Null THENs/ELSEs Included as Appropriate?

Is Each Branch Target Correct?

Is the Most Frequently Exercised Test Leg the THEN Clause?

INSPECTION SPECIFICATION
Examples of What to Examine When Looking for Errors

I_2 Interconnection Calls

For Each Interconnection Call to Either a Macro, SVC or
Another Module:

Are All Required Parameters Passed Set Correctly?

If Register Parameters Are Used, Is the Correct Register Number
Specified?

If Interconnection Is a Macro,

Does the Inline Expansion Contain All Required Code?

No Register or Storage Conflicts between Macro and Calling
Module?

If the Interconnection Returns. Do All Returned Parameters
Get Processed Correctly?

Fig 26.

PROCESS OPERATIONS	RATE OF PROGRESS (LOC/HR)		OBJECTIVES OF THE OPERATION
	DESIGN I_1	CODE I_2	
1. OVERVIEW	500	--	COMMUNICATION/ EDUCATION
2. PREPARATION	80	125	EDUCATION
3. INSPECTION	130	150	FIND ERRORS
4. FOLLOW-UP	--	--	SEE THAT ALL ERRORS, PROBLEMS & CONCERNS HAVE BEEN RESOLVED

Fig 27. Inspection Process and Rate of Progress. Source: Fagan IBM TR 21.572.

The ratio of effort involved in fixing software errors early as opposed to late in development

In Fig 28 Fagan shows one reason why his method of inspection is more effective than previous software quality measurement methods.

The rule seems to be that the earlier you can find and fix a problem in software, the cheaper it will be.

Fagan attempted to measure the cost of fixing errors at different points in the process. The results he got (which were actually more like "12" and "98" than the rounded off 10 and 100 he uses in the figure; he emphasized to me that his principle was based on real measurement, and was not just a guess, as the round numbers in the illustration might imply) indicated that catching errors at source code inspection time or design time was 10 to 100 times cheaper than discovering and correcting them at early or late stages of program testing.

In addition, he makes the important point that the "point of management control over quality is moved up much earlier in the schedule". Management receives an earlier warning of potential problems, and can attempt to do something about them before they get out of control.

EFFECT OF INSPECTION ON PROCESS MANAGEMENT

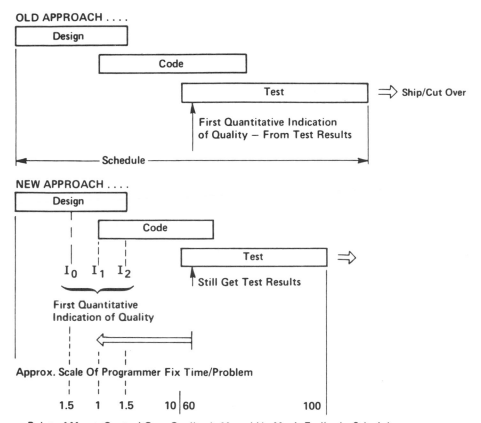

- Point of Mgmt. Control Over Quality Is Moved Up Much Earlier In Schedule.
- Error Rework At This Level Is 1/10 As Expensive.

Fig 28. From "Design and Code Inspections" (FAGAN IBM TR 21. 572).
Early inspections of design and non-compiled program code are
shown to be powerful tools for increasing programmer productivity.

Results of using test inspection

Rodney Larson, reporting (LARSON-IBM-21586) his experience with test plan inspections and test case inspections written for testing four new functions of about 20,000 lines of "PLS" language development code, wrote that:

1. About 30% additional test cases were added to the original plans.

2. 176 major errors and 254 minor errors were uncovered.

3. An 85% estimated saving in people hours resulted from the detection of the 176 major errors, as well as corresponding (unestimated) computer test time.

4. The minor errors detected resulted in additional saving.

Again, we are forced to recognize that, although many readers might be tempted to argue "I can't go around measuring everything. My programmers have too much work to do already", the introduction of appropriate measuring techniques does not <u>cost,</u> it <u>saves.</u> It is not a luxury, it is a necessity.

Just as auditing of the business accounts of limited companies is required by law in many countries, to protect investors, we might one day find that inspection of computer programs might attain a similar position. Similarly, maritime insurance companies will not "classify" and "certify" ships until a Veritas inspection of the design and later the operational ship has been carried out. These two analogies will allow the imaginative reader to consider the future of software inspections.

Details of the test inspection procedure are reproduced in Appendix B.

Motivational metrics: metric techniques which help human communication

Software metrics as a motivational technique

The chapter entitled "Reliability Metrics" gives some basic measuring concepts which are related to reliability. Bebugging and dual coding (discussed above) are illustrations of some practical instruments for actually measuring such things as reliability and maintainability.

Any improvement in our ability to measure system quality is certainly an improvement in our ability to motivate people to design, construct and maintain systems of desired quality levels.

Other measuring methods are "acceptance tests", as practiced when receiving new software and hardware packages, data-base diagnosis programs as described elsewhere in this book, and contracts for system quality as illustrated in Fig 30. This contract specification is an artificial composite based on two real software contracts I have negotiated that contained such clauses.

PORTABILITY

(= DEGREE OF NECESSARY CONVERSION)

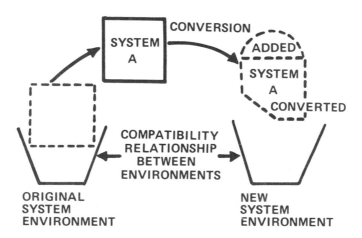

Fig 29. <u>Portability</u> is the property of a system which allows it to be moved to the new environment with relative ease.

Contract for
Software Portability

THE APPLICATION SHALL BE CONSTRUCTED SO THAT
TOTAL SYSTEM PORTABILITY IS NOT LESS THAN 95%
IN TOTAL.

THIS IMPLIES A GUARANTEE THAT THE CONSULTANT
SOFTWARE HOUSE WILL UNDERTAKE TO CONVERT TO
ANY STANDARD COBOL ENVIRONMENT OF MAJOR
MANUFACTURER FOR A MAXIMUM PRICE OF 5% (100 − 95)
OF THE ORIGINAL PROGRAMMING/DEBUGGING COST
[EXCLUSIVE SYSTEM ANALYSIS AND DESIGN].

THIS INCLUDES ALL PROGRAMS, MACHINE LANGUAGE
SUBROUTINES, CONTROL CARDS, NECESSARY SOFTWARE,
JOB OPERATIONAL SPECIFICATIONS, PHYSICAL FILE
CONVERSION AND LOGICAL FILE DATA CONVERSION.

THE OPERATIONAL COST AND RELIABILITY ARE TO
REMAIN AT THE SAME LEVEL AS FOR 100% PORTABLE
PROGRAMS AND FILES.

Fig 30. This example is based on two contracts that I negotiated, one
for an accounting system package which already existed, but
which the user wanted to be able to take over from a service
bureau for his own (at that time undetermined) computer, the
other for the production of a payroll package which predictably
had to be run on three known computers.

Clearly the "software house" is motivated by this measure of software
portability to design and construct the software (including the files and
control cards, etc.) to a predetermined level. If they fail, they have to
pay a practical and financial penalty. Notice that both performance and
reliability must be specified as constant quality parameters in such a
contract in order to avoid "cheating"; that is, to avoid the software
house simplifying the task of conversion at the expense of other system
qualities.

As a general rule, the system designer must identify all essential system qualities. A quality is essential if the project or system could fail when that particular quality was unexpectedly below a critical level. Then, by borrowing conceptual or practical metrics from other disciplines, or by inventing them, these qualities must be measured during the planning, development and operation of the system. The failure to check all quality dimensions in this manner can easily lead to project failure due either to lack of sufficient operational quality or to overexpenditure of resources to make the system operational.

Measuring the effect of programmer motivation in terms of program qualities

Fig 31 shows that the attributes of program production (the resources for making it and the resulting qualities) depend on the clarity with which the project goals are stated.

In brief, the more clearly a goal is stated and measured, the more likely the programmers are to try to satisfy that goal area. It seems that measurability has an effect on the relative priority of goals. This might explain why "planned finished date for the project" has so far had more influence on projects than "maintainability of the programs", portability and other less easy-to-measure concepts.

It is crucial for the making of a relevant system design that the goals of the design are clearly stated.

Design goals are always expressed in practical terms as multi-dimensional goals. These are usually all sub-goals of the concept of a "good" system, but it is nevertheless necessary to break down the larger and more general goals into smaller and more measurable goal concepts.

Many of the terms used to describe system goals have different meanings for different observers. It is therefore necessary, for unambiguous communication of design goal ideas, to define these goals in such a way that they can be objectively measured in practice with controllable accuracy.

The first step is often a theoretical metric, like the idea of a volt. The next step is a practical measuring device, like a magnetically driven mechanical-needle voltmeter.

The effective use of metrics is well understood in most modern engineer-

| THE PROGRAMMING GROUPS MAJOR OBJECTIVE WAS | THE RESULTING RANK WHEN PROGRAMS WERE EVALUATED (1 = best , 5 = worst) | | | | PRODUCTION TIME |
	MEMORY	CLARITY OF OUTPUT	PROGRAM	STATEMENTS	
MINIMIZE PRIMARY MEMORY NEED	1	4	4	2	5
MAXIMIZE PROGRAM OUTPUT READABILITY	5	1	1-2	5	2-3
MAXIMIZE PROGRAM SOURCE TEXT READABILITY	3	2	1-2	3	4
MINIMIZE NUMBER OF PROGRAM STATEMENTS	2	5	3	1	2-3
MINIMIZE TIME TO COMPLETE PROGRAM	4	3	5	4	1

Fig 31. Experimental results demonstrating that clearly stated objectives motivate programmers to achieve significantly different results from groups which are differently motivated. Source: G. M. Weinberg 1974, Lecture visuals, "Models of Programming Productivity". With some modifications in the text.

ing disciplines and in modern business management. There is general recognition of the fact that absence of metrics leads to lack of control over systems, and finally to failure. The fact that a particular system attribute has never been measured before, or is difficult to measure directly, or with high accuracy, does not easily discourage the trained engineer or business management consultant. If necessary the best possible practical measuring devices (contracts with acceptance tests, or plans for business growth, for example) are constructed so that some control can be maintained over progress towards the desired goals and so that people are motivated to try to attain those goals which lie behind the construction of the measures of quality.

Fig 32 illustrates some simple concepts of the practical statement of goals.

ATTRIBUTE	METRIC	LIMITS		PRIORITY INDICATION	
		MIN	MAX	%	MORE IMPORTANT THAN
ROBUSTNESS	garbage in does not lead to G. out	Common human errors detected	Any garbage is corrected	30	Effectiveness
EFFECTIVENESS	Transactions per cost-unit	25 TRANS/ SEC 36000/hour	No upper limit	20	Security

Fig 32. An example of ways of indicating system design goal priorities.

Fig 33 gives the reader a "form" which he can use to specify his system metrics. The exercise of trying to fill out this specification is highly revealing. Firstly we discover how little training we have in doing such a vital task. Secondly, upon successful completion of the specification and its systematic use as a background for design decisions, we are bound to observe that it is a powerful tool for channeling our decision-making towards relevant designs. In short, it motivates.

TRW requirements/properties matrix

One of the institutions which seems to be most aware of the importance of multidimensional metrics is the TRW Systems Group (One Space Park, Redondo Beach, Ca 90278, USA). In their excellent publication Characteristics of Software Quality (TRW-SS-73-09, Dec 1973) they thoroughly explore the major quality metrics for software systems, as well as the practical techniques for using them and for measuring them.

Figs 34 and 35, reproduced from this book, show a simple method for relating design decisions to the multidimensional goals which have been stated prior to making more detailed design decisions.

The observant reader can get a lot of interesting ideas about the handling of reliability, maintainability and testing of systems by a careful study of these two illustrations.

The major point about the TRW requirements/properties matrix is stressed in yet another TRW publication Reliable Cost-Effective, Secure

PROGRAM ATTRIBUTE SPECIFICATION

	ATTRIBUTE	METRIC	PRIORITY			
			MIN.	MAX.	%	MORE IMPORTANT THAN ATTRIBUTE
1						
2						
3						
4						
5						
6						
7						
8						
9						
10						
11						
12						
13						

Fig 33.

Software (TRW-SS-74-14): one of the major causes of problems in regard to software production is the fact that the initial design specifications are often incomplete or inconsistent. The matrix is a tool for making control of specifications for consistency and completeness a more "visible" task. If you forgot to include something, you have a blank square staring you in the face to remind you of it.

These techniques have been developed for large-scale systems, but I believe them to be valuable as thinking tools and specification tools for very small systems (for example those using only a few weeks of human effort).

MULTIDIMENSIONAL ANALYSIS OF FUNCTIONAL REQUIREMENTS

Functional Requirement	Run speed	Storage	Input-output	Reliability	Maintainability	Growth potential	Measurability	Programming standards	Testing
1. Machine independence	B	A	D1	O	D2,3	O	O	D2,3	D4
3. Occupy <25K words of core storage	O	D5	D5	O	O	D5,6	D7	O	D7,8
3. Multisection capability	A	D9	D9	D10,11	D12	D12	O	O	D13,14
4. Multisection iteration	D15	D16,R7	D16,17	D18	D19	D19	D15	D20	D21,22

O – irrelevant or self-explanatory
A – analyzed
B – being analyzed
Di – covered by design specification Di
Rj – overlaps requirement Rj

Fig 34. Requirements/Properties Matrix

DESIGN SPECIFICATIONS FROM FUNCTION/PROPERTY TABLE

D1. Flag any installation-dependent I/0 statements with special comment card.
D2. Use standard FORTRAN.
D3. Whenever an assembly language routine is incorporated for efficiency, maintain an equivalent FORTRAN routine.
D4. Run test cases on at least two machines.
D5. Organize into a resident kernel and a library on a peripheral storage device.
D6. Provide capability for updating and expanding library.
D7. Leave room in core to accommodate measurement routines and test drivers.
D8. Test library and library update capabilities.
D9. Resident storage of section parameters must be limited or volatile.
D10. Provide means of specifying a backup condition to terminate a section if the primary condition is not reached.
D11. Provide mechanism for determining when there are no more sections to be processed.
D12. Expandable list of section termination conditions.
D13. Develop multisection test cases.
D14. Develop cases to test D10, D11, and D12.
D15. Make execution time available to user for decisions on when to terminate iteration.
D16. Limited resident storage of section parameters. Refines D9.
D17. Provide means of specifying independent and dependent variables, end condition, tolerance, and initial partial derivatives for iteration.
D18. Provide means of specifying a backup condition in case iteration doesn't converge.
D19. Expandable list of variables for iteration.
D20. Resident storage of section parameters must not be modified during execution.
D21. Develop multisection iteration test cases.
D22. Develop cases to test D15, D18, D19.

Fig 35. Design Specification List

The Mecca method: a tool for communication and motivation

The MECCA Multi-Element Component Comparison and Analysis Method

This technique, originally developed by myself in 1968 for use in describing software by means of a simple model, has already found wide practical application in several countries in the following areas:

- computer selection option comparison (including software components)

- data base management package comparison (CODASYL, Swedish Air Force)

- comparison of alternative operating systems (Fig 36)

- comparison of choices of major installation programming language (bank) (e.g. COBOL versus PL/I)

- evaluation of a decision (in a major international corporation) of whether to centralize or decentralize all its computer resources including software support.

The method is really simply a formalization of the intuitive method that systematic individuals would apply to the problem of comparing complex alternatives such as software designs. The formalization consists of the application of a number of simple principles, all of which are well known in advance, but which until recently have not been combined and taught as a tool for analyzing software attributes.

Obviously, although the MECCA method can be used together with rather informal and subjective measures (in fact, in the absence of better metrics and measuring tools there is often no alternative to less stringent data) the application of the measuring concepts and tools discussed elsewhere in this book will improve the accuracy and credibility of the MECCA model.

The working steps should be simple to understand using Fig 36 and the supporting illustrations. In Appendix C there is a several-page MECCA model as an example, together with a sample of how the data collection form is used to note references to software attributes, prior to making a comparative point evaluation. (App. D).

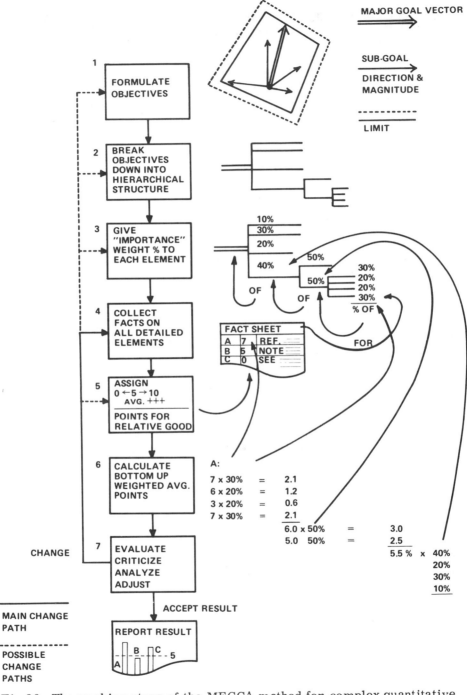

Fig 36. The working steps of the MECCA method for complex quantitative comparison.

Collecting the basic data

The following form (MECCA Element Data Collection Form in Fig 37) is convenient for noting the characteristics for each of the alternatives, at the level of the most "elementary" (in the COBOL sense of the word) items in the MECCA model, which is where the most detailed evaluations are carried out.

The kind of data noted here may for example be:

- references to contract guarantees

- references to actual measures of storage use or performance tests of software

- references to manuals, handbooks, sales offers

- noted claims or counter-claims from sales meetings with software sales representatives

- facts or interpretations of facts

- user experiences with the particular software system

The MECCA point calculation form

The MECCA Point Calculation Form (Fig 38) is convenient for noting the structure of the multi-level model.

In addition the elementary level points are noted here and weight times point calculation may be made and thereafter pushed up to the next, higher, level of the model, until the top level is reached.

Large computer evaluation models have had 300 to 400 elements in all. Programs have been written by individual users to do arithmetic, re-computation and presentable reporting of the results, as well as analysis of sensitivity to change in the evaluations of the model.

However, for most practical purposes, a computerized model is not necessary, since it is often more convenient to make alterations with pencil and paper. The hierarchical structure means that even low-level modifications do not impact more than a small part of the calculations already carried out. This makes it convenient to examine alternative evaluations.

MECCA: ELEMENT DATA-COLLECTION FORM		project no. :
system :	written by :	chapter/sect. :
subsystem :		page :
prev. issue :	approved by :	issued :

Config. A	**Decision documentation** [1]
Points	

Config. B	**Decision documentation** [1]
Points	

Config. C	**Decision documentation** [1]
Points	

Config. D	**Decision documentation** [1]
Points	

[1] Give references to manuals (page no.) to save space here. All entries not made by "written by"-person must be initialed.

Fig 37.

MECCA: POINT CALCULATION FORM

system   :
subsystem :
prev. issue :

written by   :

approved by :

project no.   :
chapter/sect. :
page   :
issued   :

Element no.	Next highest group element no.	Sub-level digit	Element name and comments	Group level [1]	Weight %	Configuration A Assigned points	Configuration A Weighted points	Configuration B Assigned points	Configuration B Weighted points	Configuration C Assigned points	Configuration C Weighted points	Configuration D Assigned points	Configuration D Weighted points
		0			X								
		1			X								
		2			X								
		3			X								
		4			X								
		5			X								
		6			X								
		7			X								
		8			X								
		9			X								
This is the complete element no. as used on ELEMENT DATA form			TOTAL WEIGHTED POINTS										

[1] Put G here if element will be further exploded

Fig 38.

77

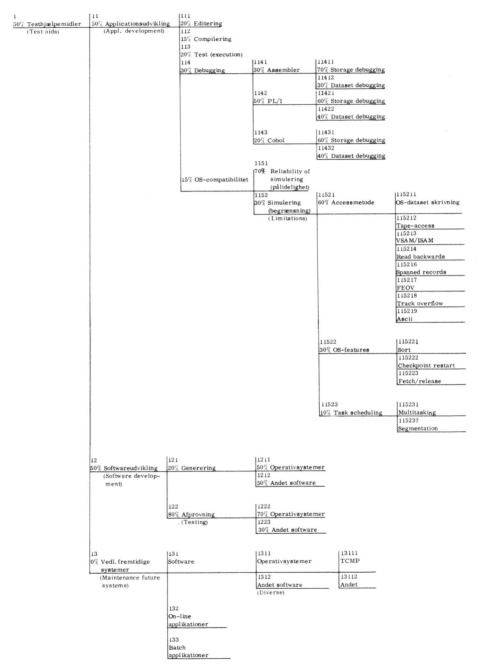

Fig 39. Actual MECCA evaluation model for operating system (unaltered page of user report). This is submodel Test Aids.

Fig 40. Table — "Test Aids" submodel of MECCA evaluation (rotated table)

FUNKTIONER	% – Weight	VM/CMS P	VM/CMS WP	TSO P	TSO WP
1 Testhjælpemidler (Test aids)	50	6.2	3.1	6.2	3.1
11 Applicationsudvikling (Applic. developm.)	50	4.3	2.2	6.3	3.2
111 Editering	20	1.1	2.0	5	0.7
112 Compilering	15			5	1
113 Test (execution)	20			5	1
114 Debugging	30	3.8	1.1	7.6	2.3
1141 Assembler	30	4.1	1.2	8	2.4
11411 Storage debugging	70	5	3.5	8	5
11412 Dataset debugging	30	2	0.6	8	2
1142 PL/1	50	3.8	1.9	6.2	4.0
11421 Storage debugging	60	5	3	5	3
11422 Dataset debugging	40	2	0.8	8	3
1143 Cobol	20	3.8	0.8	6.2	1.2
11431 Storage debugging	60	5	3	5	3
11432 Dataset debugging	40	2	0.8	8	3
115 OS-compatibilitet	15	4.2	0.6	10	1.5
1151 Simulering (pålideligh.) (Reliability of it)	70	6	4.2	10	7
1152 Simulering (begrænsning) (Limitations of it)	30	0	0	10	3
11521 Accesmetode	60	0	0	10	6
11522 OS-feature	30	0	0	10	3
11523 Task scheduling	10	0	0	10	1
12 Softwareudvikling (Softw. development)	50	8			
121 Generering	20	5	1	4.5	0.9
1211 Operativsystemer	50	5	2.5	4	2
1212 Andet software	50	5	2.5	5	2.5
122 Afprøvning (Testing)	80	8.8	7	1.2	1
1222 Operativsystemer	70	10	7	0	0
1223 Andet software	30	6	1.8	4	1.2
13 Vedl. fremtidige systemer (Maint. future syst.)	0	–	–	–	–
131 Software		–	–	–	–
1311 Operativsystemer	–	–	–	–	–
13111 TCMP	–	–	–	–	–
13112 Andet	–	–	–	–	–
13112 Andet (Diverse) Software					
132 On-line applicationer	–	–	–	–	–
133 Batch applicationer	–	–	–	–	–

(Header note: P = Point, WP = Weighted Point)

Fig 40. Point calculation for the "Test Aids" submodel of the MECCA evaluation of software (unretouched example of actual evaluation) from Danish user.

The reader is refered to my previous works on the MECCA method (GILB-2/69 and GILB-3/69, GILB-CTC-74) and Appendix C.

Use of MECCA to compare two major operating system alternatives

Figs 39 and 40 show the model used by one large Scandinavian IBM user to help decide which of two software systems ("VM/CMS" combination or TSO version (Time Sharing Option) of IBM Operating System) they should select for the short term.

The model and results are, at best, only relevant for the user in question, and any evaluation of them requires background data not supplied here. The illustrations are meant simply to give a realistic picture of the field use of this technique. Most parts of the model are not translated, since it is fairly understandable for English language readers in any case, and it is the visual impression, not the detail, which I wish to show here.

The final result is shown in Fig 41.

		VM/CMS		TSO	
FUNCTION	WEIGHT	POINTS	W x P	POINTS	W x P
TEST AIDS	50%	6.2	3.1	4.1	2.0
EXPERIENCE BASIS	30%	3.1	1.0	4.6	1.4
OUR CONFIGURATION	10%	4.0	0.4	5.2	0.5
SECURITY	5%	5.0	0.3	4.2	0.2
RESOURCE DEMANDS	5%	4.8	0.2	6.2	0.3
	100%		5.0		4.4

Fig 41.

The report concludes with a recommendation for the use of the VM/CMS version of the operating system, in spite of the fact that sufficient local experience is not yet available on the system (see line two in Fig 41 "EXPERIENCE").

Fig 40 shows the points given (on the 0 to 10 scale, where 5 means average) and the multiplication with weights, giving the final weighted result "6.2", which is then entered in the above (highest-level) part of the evaluation model.

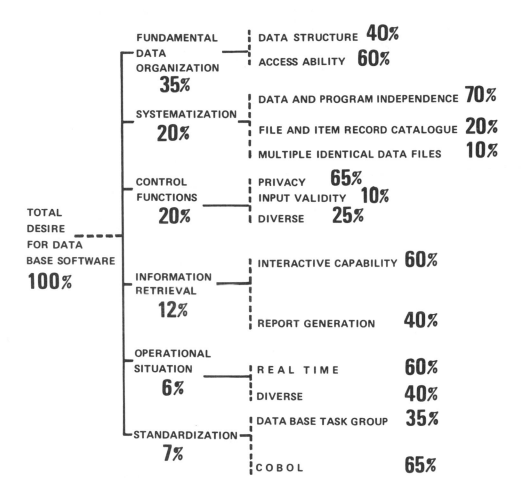

Fig 42. This is the model used to evaluate some data base management
software packages by the Swedish Military. In answer to criticism
of the validity of this model, they have pointed out that they have
substantially improved the evaluation model. Such important
factors as costs, manpower resources, maintenance and control
over resource-consuming growth in the future are not explicitly
covered.

One of the advantages of the MECCA method is that inadequate
models are easier to criticize and modify constructively.

A good exercise would be to consider the effect of changing priorities and giving resource demands 50% and test aids 5%. The reason the weights are set as they are reflects the enormous amount of development work on on-line systems expected during the period for which the decision was taken.

MECCA RESULTS FROM A DATA BASE EVALUATION

UNIVAC	DMS 1100	31.800
ICL	NIMMS	29.420
IBM	I M S	28.860
DATASAAB	OS22DB	28.560
H I S	I D S	24.170
C D C	SYSTEM 2000	23.895
BURROUGHS	F O R T E	20.460
I B M	G I S	20.190

Fig 43. Here is an initial set of results based on the Swedish MECCA model.

Dual code: an indirect measuring technique which is also applicable to large projects

Dual code and parallel programming as a relative measuring device

The observant reader will have noticed that some software metrics are based on a comparison of different programs rather than on any direct or absolute measure. This was the case in Weinberg's experiments (see Fig 31), where five different versions of the same program were written, the difference being in "quality" rather than function. To a certain extent this was true in Gould and Drongowski's bebugging experiments (see Fig 6), where the programs differed as to bug content and input/output result documentation. These software differences in an otherwise identical set of programs were used to measure the differences in maintenance ability. If the programs had contained other differences then differences in bug-fixing time and accuracy could be attributed to peculiarities in the different programs.

Both of the above-mentioned experiments were just that, experiments. The programs were small-scale, and so was the continuity of engagement of the individual programmers. We have every reason to suspect that the results may therefore be invalid for "real" programs and programming environments.

Obviously, a large-scale experiment would be interesting, but perhaps "too costly". Several of my professional colleagues have admitted the need for measuring the effects of different variations of "structured programming" in order to confirm their public assertions about the benefits of a particular variation of it (see GILB-CACM-7502 for the challenge which resulted in this discussion), but all were quick to assert that it was impossible to do experiments on the large scale desirable. None of them, however, was aware of the economic practicality of the dual code method (see GILB-DAT-7410).

Obviously, if we could simply do our programming projects two or more times with well-planned single-cause variations each time, we could learn a lot about the large-scale project effects of various technical and management changes to the programming environment (see Fig 44).

Remarkable though it may seem, writing program code twice does not automatically result in twice the cost, time or effort.

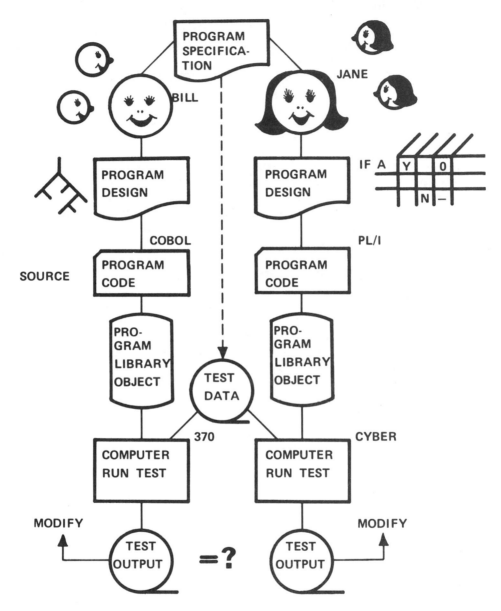

Fig 44. The use of dual code production, perhaps using parallel programmers, offers an inexpensive measuring tool for certain software variables, since the method is often necessary in any case to achieve high reliability at reasonable cost.

84

<u>The real cost of writing source code is a minor part of programming</u>
<u>cost</u>

According to various measures, the cost of writing source code has
accounted for from 5% (for military operating systems as reported to
me by Univac) to about 26% (see Fig 45). Even this "26%" is on further
analysis probably closer to less than 10% of the entire project, since
documentation (9% to 100% additional effort, according to the table) is
not included, and other overheads such as management, computer time
and the like are not clearly included as a cost.

Thus it seems safe to conclude that simply coding a program twice by
different teams of programmers should not affect the total project
effort or economics by more than 5% to 10% in the worst case. The
worst case is when no benefit in other areas of cost or work is measured.

With this observation in mind, a team at Univac (personal communication
by Univac Chief Staff Scientist Earl Joseph, May 1973) decided to write
the 20,000 statement source code of a military operating system twice,
in an effort to give themselves a tool to help debug the program more
effectively. It worked!

As you can see from the Fig 45 the test and integration phase accounts
for 30% to 50% of the programmer effort, depending largely on the
reliability demands made on the system. Thus, if the production of dual
code could either reduce the effort needed to identify bugs, or could
result in software reliability levels hitherto unobtainable using conventional methods, then it would be a case of <u>saving</u> programmer effort
by using dual code techniques.

All reported instances of dual code either report a net saving (in the
order of 15%, but the sample is very small) in resources compared to
single source code methods, or, at least, some substantial quality improvement not achievable by single code methods. An example of this
will be found in the TRW programming standard of having a FORTRAN
version coded of every machine language module, in order to enhance
portability and maintainability (see Fig 35).

In addition several users of dual code have reported that the cost of the
coding effort for two versions is <u>not</u> twice the cost of a single version,
even in terms of the coding effort.

SOFTWARE EFFORT DISTRIBUTION BY ACTIVITY

	Analysis and Design (percent)	Coding and Auditing (percent)	Test and Integration (percent)
Command-Control (SAGE, NTDS)	35	17	48
Command-Control (TRW)	46	20	34
Spaceborne (GEMINI, SATURN)	34	20	46
General Purpose Executive (OS/360)	33	17	50
Scientific (TRW)	44	26	30
Business (RAYTHEON)	44	28	28

Note: Additional effort for documentation: 9-100%.

Fig 45. Source: Barry Boehm, TRW-Systems, ref. THCOS-7309

Why dual code may be a cost-saving measuring device

THOMSON-CSF researchers report "An APL version is usually obtained in a much shorter time than with conventional ⌊I take this to mean FORTRAN: TG⌋ methods. Gains of the order of 10 are not unheard of." (DEMARS-73).

Lockheed Researchers report that "From a cost standpoint, preliminary experiments in the preparation of distinct software have shown that if one includes testing costs, then the preparation of distinct software can compare favorably with thoroughly tested conventional software modules, contrary to what intuition might lead one to expect." (FISCHLER-74).

In the case of THOMSON-CSF the main reason why the APL ("A Programming Language") program is used in addition to the FORTRAN program is:

1. To shorten the effort needed to get a comparable machine-readable logic specification, even at the expense of a longer running time (APL is only used for testing in their case anyway).

2. To get a high-level "documentation" of the FORTRAN program.

3. To reduce the probability of systematic programming code errors or compiler errors influencing the result. Lockheed refers to this as the <u>degree of distinctness</u>, which is a separate software measure.

The result is that the cost of dual code is about 110% (10% more coding cost), which can be balanced against the advantages gained in testing and program modification. In a sense, one version of the program does all the work of hand calculation or desk testing, which human testers must otherwise do in order to judge program output for correctness. Therein lies a major saving.

The objectives of the Lockheed researchers in using dual code were different. They were interested in operationally dual, but distinctly different, programs to detect software errors automatically in normal operation: "As noted in the first experiment, the effort required to develop a new version even in a different language, was minimal, mostly because the same analysis and algorithm were used, and because BASIC and FORTRAN are similar in syntax and concept. " (FISCHLER-74, pp. 4-6).

Consequently, in those situations which can probably benefit from the use of dual code in any case, we can make use of it to measure on a large scale the effects of any variables which are of current interest. It becomes a "free" experiment or measuring tool.

In another case (Skaar, Norsk Data-Elektronikk A/S, Oslo), five parallel programmers simultaneously producing independent micro-programs managed to reduce the total machine CPU timings to less than half of the time required for an original mono-coded set of micro-programs. The competitive and measured environment may, as in this case, also reduce the cost of dual code used as a metric device.

Logical complexity measurement

Practical measurement of logical complexity of a program

In an early experiment in multidimensional software measurement on a large scale, Leonard Farr and Henry J. Zagorski (in FRIELINK-65) demonstrated, among other things, that in large programs the "IF" statement density is a measure of logical complexity, which is useful since it is both easily measured by automatic means, and significantly correlated with at least one interesting metric for which it can serve as an indirect measure.

In the illustration from Farr and Zagorski's article (Fig 46b), we see 13 measures of software related to programmer productivity. Ninety-three candidate measures initially believed to be associated with the cost of programming raw data were collected. Later there were 83 independent and 15 dependent variables measured for 27 programs. Most programs were at least 10,000 to 50,000 instructions, 3 programs exceeded 300,000 instructions. After regression analysis 50 factors remained. On the basis of experience these were reduced to a "most preferred" group of 15 factors and a "satisfactory" group of 21 factors, which were analyzed further by multivariate regression analysis, which finally resulted in the weighted formulas for predicting man-months of effort for writing the programs.

Factor 11 is "the number of instructions to perform decision functions", which has a significant weighting in the third formula, which was also the most accurate. This is, simplified, an "IF"-type statement count.

I have noted that the following factors, at least, were not included (interested readers will no doubt find others): degree of maintainability, degree of portability, reliability, security, programming language, degree of modularization, degree of comments (related to maintainability, but highly measurable). It is easy to list several other candidate factors which are probably significant predictors of program cost today, but the analysis done by Farr and Zagorski still remains an isolated historical landmark in the history of software metrics.

Other efforts

The "psychological" complexity of source programs has been measured by L. Weissman (see WEISSMAN) of Toronto and by projects he inspired in Copenhagen (the PLIX programs for automatic measurement of source program difficulty).

ANALYSIS OF PROGRAMMING COST FACTORS

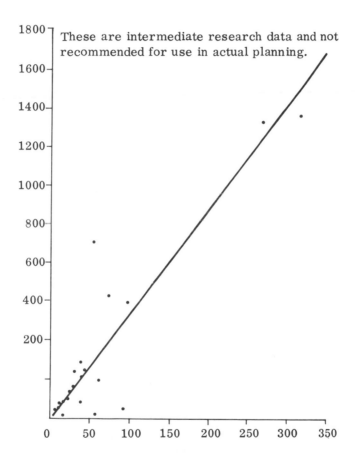

Fig 46a. Man months for program design, code, and test, versus number of machine instructions in the final program.

Equations to predict number of man months	Sample size N	Range of costs in sample	Standard error of estimate*
(1) $2.7X_1 + 121X_2 + 26X_3 + 12X_4 + 22X_5 - 497$	26	20-1500	138
(2) $2.8X_6 + 1.3X_7 + 33X_3 - 17X_8 + 10X_9 + X_{10} - 188$	24	20-900	70
(3) $8.4X_{11} + 1.8X_{12} + 18.6X_5 + 9.7X_3 - 3.7X_{13} - 42$	21	20-300	45

Definition of variables

1. Number of instructions in original estimate (in thousands)
2. Subjective rating of information system complexity (scale 1-5)
3. Number of document types delivered to customer.
4. Number of document types for internal use
5. Number of words in the data base ($\log_{10}$)
6. Number of instructions in delivered program (in thousands)
7. Number of man miles for travel (in thousands)
8. System programmer experience (average of total years of experience with the computer, language, and application)
9. Number of display consoles
10. Percent of instructions new to this program (not re-used from previous versions)
11. Number of instructions to perform decision functions (in thousands)
12. Number of instructions to perform nondecision functions (in thousands)
13. Programmer experience with this application (average number of years)   -----

Fig 46 b * The standard error of estimate is a measure of expected deviation of estimated data from actual data. Two thirds of actual costs should fall within one standard error of their predicted values. Since this measure tends to be constant throughout the cost estimation range, the relative percent of error to total cost will decrease as one proceeds from small programs to large programs. Thus, the larger programs are able to tolerate the estimating error much more readily than smaller programs. Source: L. Farr and H.J. Zagorski, "Quantitative Analysis of Computer Programming Cost Factors: A Progress Report," in Frielink (Ed.) Economics of ADP, North-Holland, 1965, pp. 174-175.

Metrics and dissemination of technology

Applying software metrics to collection and dissemination of techniques

When only a few, stable design techniques are known and used, and when these techniques are applied to a standard scale and quality of project, then there may be little need for a formal description of the expected attributes of the techniques. In this situation everybody knows from experience which techniques to use and what to expect when they are applied.

The current situation in software technology, however, is in a process of explosive change. The number of alternative techniques available for solving a single design problem is increasing rapidly. The scale of software projects undertaken has grown by orders of magnitude. The growth in the difficulty and importance of projects increases slightly faster than our competence in mastering such projects. Past experience must be transmitted to students, and in such a way that it does not become obsolete before the student realizes it and misapplies it to a real project.

In such a situation software technology must resort to the time-tested method used by most other complex disciplines. It must learn to describe alternative technologies in a multidimensional and quantified manner which is objective and accurate. Knowledge can be stored in this form and does not easily become obsolete if more accurate measures, new techniques and important exceptions are added regularly to update the store of software knowledge.

The basic format of such knowledge storing is shown in Fig 47. This format is compatible with other multidimensional design techniques such as MECCA, TRW Requirement/Properties Matrix and Multidimensional Design specification, which are discussed elsewhere in this text.

A crude table of a particular set of techniques

Fig 48 shows a crude but practical use of this concept to describe alternative record protection techniques. The properties are described approximately and some enlightenment as to interesting techniques is given. The judgements are, however, purely subjective. It is not at all clear which system design requirements they apply to: whether or not they are "good" depends entirely on the application requirements. There is no objective way of determining whether this table represents the "truth" for a particular user. It is perhaps better than no table at all, but there are dangers in disseminating this description of attributes to unsophisticated readers.

LEARNING ABOUT TECHNIQUES

TECHN. LIST	Multidimensional Attributes						
	ERROR DETEC-TION PROBAB-ILITY	ERROR CORRECT. PR.	PORTAB-ILITY	GENE-RALITY	IMPLEMENT-ATION EASE	OPERA-TIONAL COST	ETC.
T1							
T2							
T3							
T4							
T5							
T6							
.							
.							
.							
.							
.							
.							
.							
T-last							

Fig 47.

TECHNIQUE	MULTIDIMENSIONAL ATTRIBUTE ANALYSIS TABLE				
	secondary	cpu	applicability	auto error	auto error
	SPACE	SPEED	GENERAL	DETECT	CORRECT
BACK UP FILE	NONE ON LINE	WORST	ALL NON TIME-CRITICAL	UPDATE PROBLEM	POSSIBLE
COMPLETE RECORD DUPLICATION	WORST 100% ON-LINE		HIGH	VERY GOOD	BEST
SELECTIVE RECORD DUPLICATION	VARIABLE	VARIABLE	GOOD	ONLY SELECTED RECORDS	ONLY SELECTED RECORDS
FIELD LEVEL LOGICAL CONTROL	EXCELLENT	BAD TO WORST	WORST	FAIR	NOT SO GOOD HIGHLY VARIABLE
RECORD LEVEL HASH TOTAL	CA. 1–2% INCREASE	COSTLY (MAY OVERLAP I/O)	VERY HIGH	VERY GOOD	LIMITED TO CON-FIRMATION
SELECTIVE R L H T	EXTRA FIELD IN RECORD	GOOD	POOR	ONLY SELECTED FIELDS	HIGHER PROB. THAN TOTAL RLHT
SELECTIVE CRITICAL FIELD DUPLICATION	1 to 5% INCREASE	GOOD	POOR	»	VERY HIGH FOR THOSE FIELDS
COMBINATIONS OF ABOVE TECHNIQUES	IN GENERAL: BEST EFFECT AND HIGH ANALYSIS AND DESIGN COST				

WARNING: THIS TABLE IS INTUITIVE AND HIGHLY DEPENDENT UPON THE PARTICULAR DESIGN CHOSEN.

THE MAIN POINT IS THAT THERE ARE A NUMBER OF ALTERNATIVE TECHNIQUES and THAT THEY MUST BE ANALYSED MULTIDIMENSIONALLY AND IN COMBINATION WITH ONE ANOTHER AND OTHER TECHNIQUES.

Fig 48. Source: Early DATA DESIGN manuscript and teaching aids (Gilb, unpublished).

<u>A more objective table</u>

Fig 49 is an improvement in that much of the data is objectively verifiable. Whether or not these qualities are "good" or "bad" is a matter of opinion which is left entirely to the designer using the table. Naturally, this particular table can stand considerable improvement, but the improvement is likely to be systematic, and in the direction of more accurate measures and a more detailed breakdown of technique variations.

In any case, students must be taught:

- to insist that knowledge be collected and presented in this form if at all possible

- to themselves organize their knowledge in this form

- to make use of such tables and related formulas for calculation of their specific design alternatives

- to understand that they must test the truth of the contents of such tables in their own particular case. Real life is complex and exceptions abound.

DATA ELEMENT DESIGN ATTRIBUTES

DATA ELEMENT DESIGN ALTERNATIVE		Probability: random error detection using self-contained algorithm		Pr. error correction using algorithm (no files/large tables)	Pr. error detection by file/table comparison	Pr. error correction via file/table data	Human sense error detection/correction Pr.	Relative CPU energy to convert − integer			
		ALGORITH. ERROR		FILE ERROR				Redundancy of combinations			
Ref.	Datametric Notation	DET.	COR.	DET.	COR.	DET. COR.	T	& inf.	COST	Refer to	
1A	**IDENTIFIERS/DESCRIPTORS**										
1A2	**NUMERIC**										
1A1a	Numeric Identifier	.0	.0	.0−.1	.0−.01	.0−.05	1	0−100 +	1		
1A1b	Self-checking	.91−.9999	.1−.9999	.0−.990	.0−.01	.0	2	10+	1.2		
1A1c	Random Spread	.0	.0	.9−.99	.08	.0	1	10−100+	1		
1A1d	Duplication	.9990	.5	.9999	.5	.7	1	1 mill.	2.1		
1A2	**ALPHANUMERIC**							d^{10} $(cP^{\ })$			
1A2a	Check Word	.0	.0	.9667−.9999987	.999 .9999	.01 .50	1	30 to 810000	1.5 → 3		
1A2b	Word Code	.0	.0	.9−.99	.90−.96	.8 .98	20−150	2.5 m	2 → 3		
1A2c	Humanized	.0	.0	.9999+	.3 .9	.9 .7	5−400+	1,000 16 mill	2 → 5		
1A2d	Self-identifying	.0	.0	.90 .99	.3 .9999	.01 .98	3 20	−	3 → 4		
1B	**QUANTIFIERS**										
1B1	Whole Nos./Integers	.0	.0	.0−.1	.0	.0 .05	1	0−5+	1	1A2d exception	
1B2	Decimal point Nos.	.0	.0	.0−.1	.0	.0 .05	5	0−5+	2.5		
1B3	Fractions	.0	.0	.0−.9	.0−.9	.0−.5	12	0	2		
1B4	Non-decimal system	.0	.0	.0−+	.0−+	.0−+	11	0−+	4		
1B5	Alphabetic Quantif.	.97−.999	.985−.99	.97 .999	.985−.99	.99	30	900−27,000	5−6		
1B6	Internal Formats	.0	.0	.0	.0	.0	2	0 to +			
1C	**NON-CHARACTER**										
1C1	Positional	(takes actual element property)					20	1−10			
1C2	Implicit	not applicable					3	0−10			
1C3	Default	»	»				3	0−1.1			
1C4	Graphical	»	»				200	0.5−3			

TABLE 1: Summary of some key properties of data element formats.
(Rough estimates, often subjective and always general)

Abbreviations
c = characters in symbol set (10 for numerics and 40 alphanumerics)
p = symbol positions, length of element
d = number of digits in the number

NOTES:
1 When two values are given, they are typical extreme (lower/upper estimate) values
when one value is given, it is a typical value and deviation from it is small

2 The "cost" column is average gross relative cost in human & machine energy for processing the data element to
first detection/correction/acceptance − it does not include savings from reliability/productivity advantages.

Fig 49. Source: Gilb, DATA DESIGN (unpublished manuscript) July 1972.

Automating software measurement

Software that reads and measures software

So far we have mainly discussed practical measuring techniques which depend for their application mainly on human effort and judgement, although several of them are subject to automation (such as <u>bebugging</u> and <u>dual code</u> error detection and recording), and MECCA has used computer programs to summarize and report results.

Most software is by nature computer-readable, or can be put in computer-readable form (for example documentation recorded as comments, and pseudo code written in a language such as APL rather than in a non-executable logical specification).

Fig 50 gives an overview of some of the tools in use (December 1973) at one advanced software house (TRW-Systems) which makes use of programs that read programs.

All of these programs are concerned with either

- providing additional documentation as required by TRW standards

or

- measuring the degree to which specific software quality measures are satisfied in the source code, comments and test data (marked * in the table).

TRW, as can be seen by a detailed examination of their publication "Characteristics of Software Quality" (TRW-SS-73-09) have tried to break down the more general characteristics of a metric, such as "structuredness", into more practical and detailed criteria for measuring their presence.

As with the MECCA method discussed earlier, the key to measurement of broad quality concepts is to break down the concepts into their component parts, and to keep on breaking down these parts until a simple measurable factor is identified. The sum of all such measures gives us a measure of the higher level qualities.

Value of (automated) metrics

TRW concludes a detailed quantitative analysis of the value of the use of metrics and concludes that the cost of applying metrics (at present) per phase and per error type is 50.19% of the cost of conventional testing. TRW concludes: "under the assumptions above, one can conclude that if metrics can be applied for less than 50.19% of the cost of conventional testing, they would be worthwhile." (TRW-SS-73-09 pp. 5-42). Obviously automation is the key to satisfying this requirement for the profitable use of metrics.

Systematic evaluation of elementary level metrics by TRW

Fig 51 is a sample of a large number of such tables in "Characteristics of Software Quality" (TRW-SS-73-09), where a searching inquiry was made for into suitable ways of measuring software quality. The work was originally done for the National Bureau of Standards, Washington D. C.

In the example the major metric structuredness is broken down into candidate measuring tools which we could term "elementary level" metrics, since they form the bottom level, and these are the criteria which TRW is investigating as the direct measuring tool.

Structuredness is one of 12 low-level metrics, the others being: device independence, completeness, accuracy, consistency, device efficiency, accessibility, communicativeness, self-descriptiveness, conciseness, legibility and augmentability.

These low-level metrics are assumed to be related to a higher level of metrics: portability, reliability, efficiency, human engineering, testability, understandability and modifiability.

And these are assumed to be related to "as-is utility" and "maintainability", which give the highest level "general utility" (Figure 3-1 TRW-SS-73-09).

Clearly, TRW recognizes five levels of metrics, including the elementary level metric concepts. This is comparable with Figs 68 and 69.

Some of the explanations of the codes used in Fig 51 will give a broader view of the way in which candidate metrics were evaluated.

AUTOMATED SOFTWARE TOOLS AND THEIR RELATION TO SOFTWARE PRODUCTION
GUIDELINES AND METRICS

Fig 50

Program Name	Implementation Level [1]	Guideline/Metric Application Paragraph Reference	Description	Remarks
DOCEDT	1	Requirements and any other specification documents maintenance and update (5.1.1.1 – 5.1.5)	Provides capability to generate and maintain a document on tape. The document is initially generated on punched cards, and then maintained on tape with corrections and additions incorporated by use of DOCEDT change cards.	Used actively in Mission Trajectory Control Project NASA/JSC FORTRAN V. UNIVAC 1108. Straight-forward convertibility to another standard FORTRAN environment.
COMPSIM	II	Design phase (5.1.2)	Uses generalized simulation system SALSIM to simulate computer system models, including user-supplied hardware models, applications software models, a software executive model, and a system environment model.	Specific applications have been made to NASA/JSC projects. UNIVAC 1108. IBM 360/370 and XDS-SIGMA 5. Similar to SPRINT which is usable on the CDC 6500 in a time-sharing mode.
PPE	II	Coding and checkout, development testing (5.1.3.1.4), DE-1.	Identifies time-consuming areas of program code or other characteristics that result in inefficient running times.	Used in IBM 360/370 with OS/MV 7 executive.

*

98

Name	Class	Phase	Function	Remarks
*TAFIRM	III	Coding and checkout (5. 1.3) CP-3. CP-6. AR-	Checks executability and accuracy of computations for small logical units of code. Requires developer to structure programs into logical testable units.	Used on the CDC 3800 for JOVIAL J4 programs, with the System IIB operating system. Similar to ASIST-I, usable in the XDS-SIGMA 5.
FLOWGEN	I	Coding and checkout development testing (5.1.3, 5.1.4).	Generates program flow-charts from FORTRAN source input.	Used on CDC 6500 (time sharing version) and UNIVAC 1108. The former version was modified to leased CALCOMP version to handle larger programs and provide paginated output.
DEPCHT	I	Coding and checkout, development and integration testing, system testing, operations and maintenance (5.1.3 - 5.1.5) CP-4.	Generates in list format crossreferences of referenced subroutines and vice-versa, and in chart format, a description of program linkages originating from a user-specified "element-of-origin."	Used in Mission Trajectory Control Project NASA/JSC, FORTRAN V. UNIVAC 1108.
BLKGEN/SPECPN	I	Coding and checkout, development and integration testing, system testing, operations and maintenance (5.1.3 - 5.1.5) SD-5.	Define and maintain COMMON data structures for large FORTRAN programs	Used in Mission Trajectory Control Project NASA/JSC, FORTRAN V. UNIVAC 1108. This capability is standard in JOVIAL J4 environment where it is called the COMPOOL capability.

*	DPNDCY	I	Coding and checkout, development and integration testing, system testing, operations and maintenance (5.1.3 – 5.1.5) CP-11.	Performs a consistency analysis on inputs to the COMMON data base. Printout shows cross-references of variable names to subroutines and vice-versa. Errors or inconsistencies are identified.	Used with BLKGEN/SPECPN on FORTRAN V. UNIVAC 1108.
	FREF	I	Coding and checkout, development and integration testing, system testing, operations and maintenance (5.1.3 – 5.1.5) CS-10.	Generates cross-reference listing of statement numbers and offset, variable names, array names and function names. Codes indicating usage of the name are given.	Available on CDC-6500 in time-sharing mode for FORTRAN IV programs. BREF similar for BASIC language.
	FSEQ[2]	I	Coding and checkout, development and integration testing, system testing, operations and maintenance	Resequences the statement label (numbers) in a FORTRAN source program in ascending order: also helps to flag FORMAT statements by making the last digit of the statement number a "2."	Available on CDC-6500 in time-sharing mode.

* CODE AUDITOR	II	Coding and checkout, development and integration testing, system testing, operations and maintenance (5. 1. 5) SD-1, ST-3, LG-5, ST-5, ST-2, DE-2.	Provides automated standards evaluation of FORTRAN source code.	Actively used on CDC 7600 for Site Defense Project Currently being modified to evaluate expanded list of programming standards.
* TDEM	I	Development testing (5. 1. 4). SD-5, SD-6,	Measures effectiveness of test cases by generating data showing which branches of FORTRAN source code have been exercised, logically related segments and test frequencies for all segments and branches.	Used actively in Mission Trajectory Control Project NASA/JSC, FORTRAN V. UNIVAC 1108. Other related programs operate on different systems: PACE 1, CDC 6600, 7600, NODAL, CDC 6000 (time-sharing mode): TATTLE. CDC 3800 on JOVIAL J4.
* ATDG	III	Development testing (5. 1. 4).	Identify execution paths and generate optimal test cases for FORTRAN code modules (subroutines).	A prototype version is available and is undergoing test and evaluation. Used with FORTRAN V on the UNIVAC 1108.
TCOCO	III	Integration testing, system testing, operations and maintenance phases (5. 1. 4 - 5. 1. 5)	Software configuration control system for large systems.	Used with CDC 3800 on JOVIAL JOVIAL J4. An implementation of GIM, a generalized information management system which is being used directly to build configuration control systems for other computer systems.

Notes: (1) Implementation Level:

I (a) Coded program implemented and tested in some language and operating system used by TRW.
  (b) Programmers Guide and Program User's Guide are availabile.
  (c) Up-to-date configuration control for code and documentation maintained.

II (a) Same as I(a).
  (b) Use requires assistance of program developer or equivalent.
  (c) Informal configuration control of documentation and code.

III (a) Prototype version of program available
  (b) Incomplete documentation.

* = measuring software

102

Metric number	Original metric number	Definition of metrics to measure structuredness	Correlation with quality	Potential benefit	Quantifi- ability	Ease of developing automated evaluation	Complete- ness of automated evaluation
1	10.13*	Have the rules for transfer of control between modules been established and followed?	A	5	AL	E	P
2	10.12*	Are the modules limited in size?	AA	4	AL	E	P
3	1.14*	Has the ordering: commentary header block, specification statements, then executable code been followed?	A	3	CC	E	C
4	7.11*	Do all subprograms contain at most, one point of exit?	AA	4	AL	E	C
5	10.9*	Do all subprograms and functions have only one entry point?	A	4	AL	E	C
6	10.8(*)	Is program flow always forward, with commented exceptions?	AA	4	AL	M	P
7	10.11	Is the overlay structure consistent with the subprogram's sequencing?	A	5	ER		
8	6.8	Is the program subdivided into modules in accordance with readily recognized functions?	A	5	TR		
9	4.7*	Is the program written in a standard set of constructs available in the particular programming language used (preferably a national standard such as ANSI)?	AA	4	CC	E	P

Fig 51. Evaluated Attributes of the Metrics Measuring the Primitive Characteristic – Structuredness (ST)
Source: TRW

An explanation of elementary level metric evaluation by TRW

In the second column of Fig 51, an asterisk is placed against all metrics which rated high on all of the 5 evaluation areas on the right-hand side. Exceptional satisfaction of these criteria rated an asterisk in parentheses.

From this we can see that metric 6, measurement of forward flow of the logic with "commented exceptions" is a highly measurable criterion.

Here is a list of the codes used in the other columns.

Correlation with software quality:

A = Always a non-negative correlation between high score for the metric and possession of the associated primitive characteristic.
AA = Almost Always the above correlation.
U = Usually the above correlation.
S = Sometimes the above correlation.

Potential benefit:

5 = Extremly important for metric to be satisfied; major potential troubles if not.
4 = Important for metric to be satisfied.
3 = Fairly important for metric to be satisfied.
2 = Some incremental value for metric to be satisfied.
1 = Slight value, no real loss if not.

Quantifiability:

AL = Can be done cost effectively via an automated ALgorithm.
CC = Can be done cost-effectively via an automated Compliance Checker if given a checklist.
UR = Requires an Untrained human Reader.
TR =   "   a Trained human Reader.
ER =   "   an Expert human Reader.
EX =   "   the program to be EXecuted.

Ease of developing automated evaluation

E = Easy, M = Medium difficulty, D = Difficult

Completeness of automated evaluation

C - Total, P = Partial, I = Inconclusive results.

The reader should now be in a position to understand the table in Fig 51. The table also gives an idea of the groundwork necessary before automated measurement of software attributes is possible.

Examination of the table tells us that TRW believes that the degree of structuredness of a program is highly susceptible to automated evaluation of the measurement of the most important elementary level characteristics of "structuredness". Finally, we have a measuring instrument for the question: How structured is this program?

In the TRW work described above, structuredness was related to both "testability" and "understandability", which again were sub-levels of maintainability. The result is an approach to a priori prediction of the maintainability of a program, which can also be measured by methods discussed previously such as bebugging.

I remember some of the TRW people telling me in 1974 that they had tools for automatic measurement of about one half of the metric concepts, at that time. They hoped by the end of 1975 to have fully automated the measurement of all important metrics!

Whether or not they achieve this result, the intent is clear, and the optimistic outlook for the automation of software metrics (based on a detailed study and the extensive experience cited above) makes this field well worth watching.

The question is no longer whether we can measure software qualities at all, but how accurately and how cheaply we can automate the process.

Automated aid to early detection of errors (TRW) contrasted with inspection

TRW has developed a piece of software called Minuteman Operational Software Simulation, consisting of both on-line and interactive test aids to:

- facilitate user construction of test sequences

- determine expected results

- simulate the environment

- generate message traffic

- check generated message traffic

- verifies interface timing and responses

- provide diagnostic features.

Some, but not all of these features are of a software measurement category. The "simulation" of the software environment makes possible extensive software analysis aids which are "unavailable in the test bed [the real hardware environment] and provide a powerful capability for the rapid isolation of program coding errors."

The effect of using the tool is illustrated in Fig 52, which we must assume was for comparable efforts. The use of MOSS resulted in a higher initial error-finding rate and a cleaner system in later stages.

This example is a clear indication of the power of automated aids for helping us measure error content in software. Notice, however, that all these test phases are after the human inspection phases used by Fagan of IBM (I-1 and I-2) discussed earlier. They are in fact at the test phase where inspection I-3 was used, and proved counter-productive (see earlier in this text) since the earlier inspections had caught most of the errors. As far as I can determine from TRW and IBM, they were unaware of the details of each other's work. I suspect that IBM would argue: "Why bother to find all those errors at such a late stage when with early inspections you can save 10 to 100 times the correction effort?". TRW might reply: "You still have to test the programs and you might as well do it with the best automated tools available."

My guess is that both of these advanced developments, early inspection, and automated error detection and testing aids, will be used together in the future.

Automated test path analysis: measurement of test case completeness

Several organizations have begun to produce programs that analyze the execution sequences the program goes through. Most prominent among these is the General Research Corporations Program Validation Project, which has resulted in a commercially available set of programs for the analysis of FORTRAN programs (RXVP, ref. GRC, 5383 Hollister Ave, Santa Barbara, CA for details and papers)

HOW SUCCESSFUL WAS MOSS ?

FIRST VERSION (WITHOUT MOSS)
HARDWARE TEST BED

MODULE TESTING	INTEGRATED TESTING	DEVELOPMENT TESTING	SYSTEM TESTING
125 ERRORS	35 ERRORS	451 ERRORS	103 ERRORS

SECOND VERSION (WITH MOSS)
HARDWARE TEST BED

MODULE TESTING	INTEGRATED TESTING	DEVELOPMENT TESTING	SYSTEM TESTING
234 ERRORS	54 ERRORS	44 ERRORS	(NOT COMPLETED YET)

Fig 52. Source: TRW-SS-74-14 pp. 5-94.

TRW-Systems has also worked on this technology (TRW-SS-73-01 and TRW-SS-74-14 pp. 6-52) which has resulted in the NODAL (Node Determination and Analysis Program) software. NODAL "automatically instruments the software code to determine which path segments have been exercised in a series of tests".

Fig 53 shows this. Two measures are given that are of interest in software metrics technology:

1. The test effectiveness ratio (85% and 100% of the 34 segments in the example were executed).

2. The frequency of execution of each segment. Useful for optimization, balancing test cases, and detecting unexpected program path use. Notice particularly the "0"s in the first set.

A "segment" here is the sequence of logical instructions between a starting instruction in a sequence and a logical fork or branch point.

At TRW the NODAL program is also operated with machine language programs. NODAL is being used on "Minuteman" (rocket defense) and "Site Defense Program".

SEGMENT EXECUTION FREQUENCY MAP WITH SUBROUTINE TEST
EFFECTIVENESS RATIOS (TER)

S2GKS (TER =.85)
(SEGMENTS 1-34)

	Segment	(1)	(2)	(3)					(8)	(9)
	(10)	4	3	2	0	1	2	0	2	1
	2	0	2	16	4	0	15	6	1	14
FOUR TEST	15	15	3	4	0	16	7	2	14	15
CASES RUN	16	25	3	4	4					
					(34)					

SEGMENT EXECUTION FREQUENCY MAP WITH SUBROUTINE TEST
EFFECTIVENESS RATIOS (TER)

S2GKS (TER = 1. 00)
(SEGMENTS 1-34)

		6	5	4	2	1	3	1	2	1
	3	1	2	16	4	1	16	7	2	14
SIX TEST	15	16	4	5	1	17	8	2	15	16
CASES RUN	17	25	4	6	6					

Fig 53. Source: TRW-SS-74-14 pp. 6-56.

The General Research Corporation RXVP Test Path Analyzer

Figs 54-57 indicate the scope of the first commercially available
FORTRAN test path analysis tool, RXVP, "RX" meaning "prescription"
and VP "Verification of Path/Program", I imagine[*].

I understand from GRC that they are planning to make a similar tool for
COBOL programs, the background being that the U. S. Air Force has
funded this project and it has a lot of COBOL programs too.

As the reader can see, there are some analysis reports which are aimed
at giving test case construction assistance. This falls short of the objective of providing automatic test case generation based on the source
code, which has met some problems in finding a suitable theoretical or

---

[*] The original package was called RSVP, Research Software Validation
Package.

pragmatic approach. Researchers currently expect to find a breakthrough in the near future. This implies automatic construction of test cases, which would at least make sure of thorough exercising of a source program. However, the test cases would necessarily reflect errors in the source program, and hopefully we shall find suitable automatic ways of detecting that too.

E. F. Miller (Director of the GRC Program Validation Project) remarked at his 1974 Eurocomp presentation of the GRC research, that in the initial test of this product on GRC's own programmers, a group of 26 programs, which had been human inspected and were already "approved" as having met the minimum criterion that 100% of all test paths were exercised at least once, "and when every possible outcome of each program decision statement has occurred at least once" (MILLER-EURO-74) were examined by RXVP. Then, according to Miller, the RXVP program showed that 23 of the 26 programs (for which this 100% testing was supposed to be true) had had less than 80% of such paths tested! The authors were at first indignant, until they were challenged to disprove the RXVP documentation on untested paths. They gave up, of course.

This example illustrates the strength of automated tools compared with well-intentioned humans. The human "inspection" process described by Fagan should probably be augmented by such aids. The inspectors should determine whether the test path program has been used, and should not have to evaluate test completeness manually.

AN OVERVIEW OF RXVP

This page summarizes the capabilities of RXVP and shows how it is used in the testing process. The following pages describe each of the components of the RXVP system in more detail.

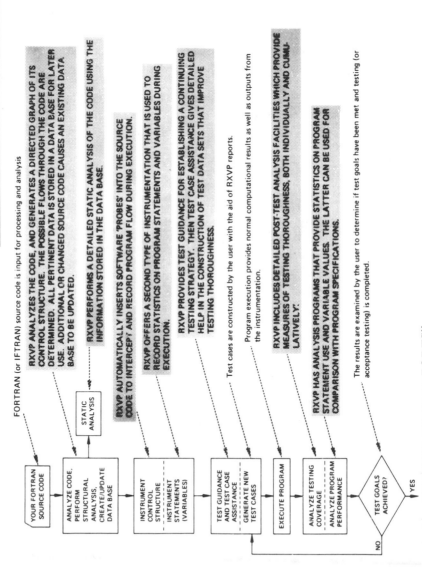

FORTRAN (or IFTRAN) source code is input for processing and analysis

RXVP ANALYZES THE CODE, AND GENERATES A DIRECTED GRAPH OF ITS CONTROL STRUCTURE. THE POSSIBLE FLOWS THROUGH THE CODE ARE DETERMINED. ALL PERTINENT DATA IS STORED IN A DATA BASE FOR LATER USE. ADDITIONAL OR CHANGED SOURCE CODE CAUSES AN EXISTING DATA BASE TO BE UPDATED.

RXVP PERFORMS A DETAILED STATIC ANALYSIS OF THE CODE USING THE INFORMATION STORED IN THE DATA BASE.

RXVP AUTOMATICALLY INSERTS SOFTWARE 'PROBES' INTO THE SOURCE CODE TO INTERCEPT AND RECORD PROGRAM FLOW DURING EXECUTION.

RXVP OFFERS A SECOND TYPE OF INSTRUMENTATION THAT IS USED TO RECORD STATISTICS ON PROGRAM STATEMENTS AND VARIABLES DURING EXECUTION.

RXVP PROVIDES TEST GUIDANCE FOR ESTABLISHING A CONTINUING TESTING STRATEGY. THEN TEST CASE ASSISTANCE GIVES DETAILED HELP IN THE CONSTRUCTION OF TEST DATA SETS THAT IMPROVE TESTING THOROUGHNESS.

Test cases are constructed by the user with the aid of RXVP reports.

Program execution provides normal computational results as well as outputs from the instrumentation.

RXVP INCLUDES DETAILED POST-TEST ANALYSIS FACILITIES WHICH PROVIDE MEASURES OF TESTING THOROUGHNESS, BOTH INDIVIDUALLY AND CUMULATIVELY.

RXVP HAS ANALYSIS PROGRAMS THAT PROVIDE STATISTICS ON PROGRAM STATEMENT USE AND VARIABLE VALUES. THE LATTER CAN BE USED FOR COMPARISON WITH PROGRAM SPECIFICATIONS.

The results are examined by the user to determine if test goals have been met and testing (or acceptance testing) is completed.

YOUR FORTRAN SOURCE CODE

ANALYZE CODE, PERFORM STRUCTURAL ANALYSIS, CREATE/UPDATE DATA BASE

STATIC ANALYSIS

INSTRUMENT CONTROL STRUCTURE
INSTRUMENT STATEMENTS (VARIABLES)

TEST GUIDANCE AND TEST CASE ASSISTANCE
GENERATE NEW TEST CASES

EXECUTE PROGRAM

ANALYZE TESTING COVERAGE
ANALYZE PROGRAM PERFORMANCE

TEST GOALS ACHIEVED?

NO

YES

Fig 54. "SAMPLE RXVP REPORTS"

110

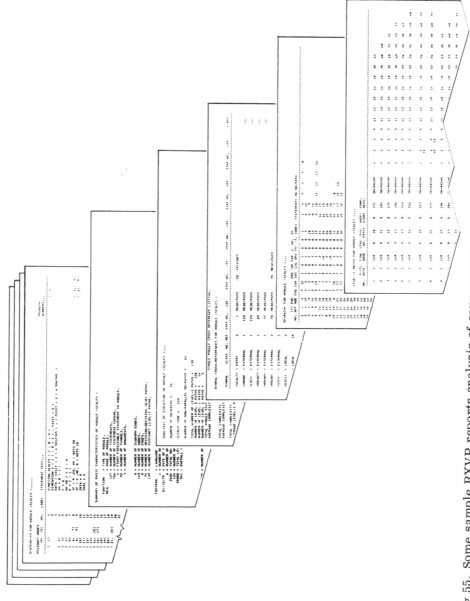

Fig 55. Some sample RXVP reports analysis of source program.

111

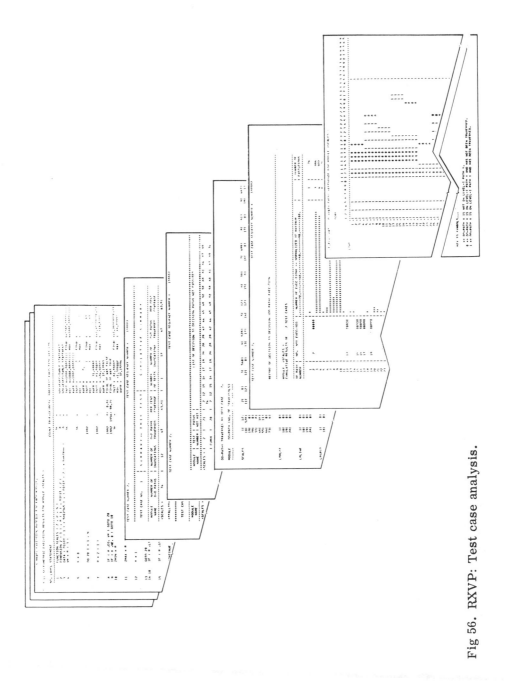

Fig 56. RXVP: Test case analysis.

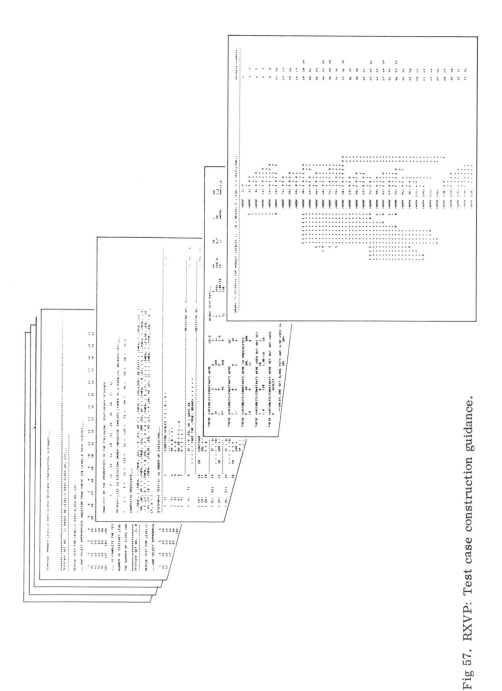

Fig 57. RXVP: Test case construction guidance.

Self-metric software at McDonnell Douglas

L. G. Stucki of McDonnell Douglas Astronautics Company described a tool which is similar in some respects to the test path analysis tools at TRW and GRC described earlier (STUCKI-IEEE-73). In a number of respects, however, it is quite different.

Firstly, it is not primarily concerned with the test path variations themselves. It concentrates on collecting data by instrumenting the activity of individual instructions. Fig 58a shows points at which additional instructions are inserted, by means of a macro-generator, into the source program. This is entirely automatic and requires no human judgement.

Fig 58b ("PET" means Program Evaluator and Tester) shows results which a programmer might use during debugging. Of particular interest is the recording of minimum and maximum values (or the first and last in the case of DO loop control variables) for assignment statements.

The impossible branch (to 530) was detected in a two-year-old program by this analysis. Human programmers were unaware of it.

In Fig 58c a measure of the degree of program documentation is given by the COMMENT count. The complexity of the module is given roughly by its size and the number of branch statements (see Farr and Zagorski earlier).

The Sample Module Timing Summary, combined with module execution frequencies from the Sample Module Summary Report (Figs 58 c & d) gives valuable hints to programmers who are trying to optimize performance of programs by improving the most critical modules.

The Test Effectiveness Statistics Fig 58f were run on 40,869 statements of old programs which had gone into operation without the benefit of this tool, on the basis of this test data, which covered only 44.5% of the executable source statements and only 35.1% of the branches. Stucki remarks that he fears that this lack of even the most elementary form of testing is common. Coding Standard violations are also measured, as two of the illustrations show.

The software was developed so that it will work on any ASA Standard FORTRAN IV compiler. The execution time increase for the instrumentation was 25% to 150%. The additional primary memory space needed varies widely depending on the type of measurement required. During 1975 additional instrumentation work was done with PET for measuring formal "assertion" accordance and for using these principles for COBOL (STUCKI-750612).

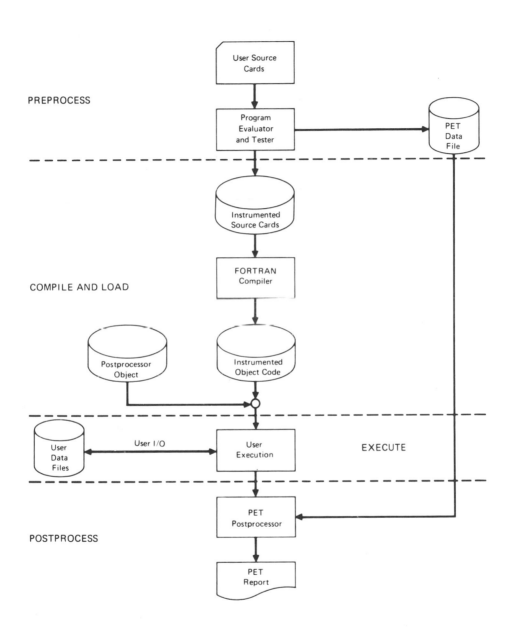

Fig 58. Program Evaluator and Tester (PET) Job Flow

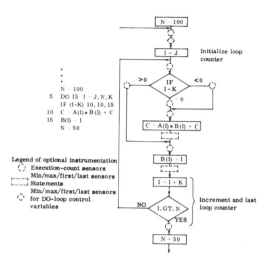

N = 100

I = J — Initialize loop counter

```
         .
         .
         .
    N = 100
  5 DO 15  I = J,N,K
    IF (I-K) 10,10,15
 10 C = A(I) * B(I) + C
 15 B(I) = I
    N = 50
```

IF I-K   >0   <0   0

C = A(I) * B(I) + C

B(I) = I

I = I + K

I.GT.N   NO / YES — Increment and last loop counter

N = 50

Legend of optional instrumentation
◇ Execution-count sensors
▢ Min/max/first/last sensors
⌐ ⌐ Statements
◇ Min/max/first/last sensors for DO-loop control variables

Fig 58a. FORTRAN Program Segment Showing Optional Instrumentation.
Source: STUCKI-IEEE-73.

ORIGINAL SOURCE CODE LISTING	EXECUTION COUNT	BRANCH COUNTS, TRUTH VALUES, MIN/MAX/FIRST/LAST VALUES
PROGRAM LISTING (LEADING V INDICATES CONVERSION WARNINGS)	COUNT	SPECIFIC EXECUTION DATA
IF(I .EQ. NUM1) GO TO 380	3793	TRUE 117 FALSE 3673
IF(ABS(S) .GT. ABS(C)) GO TO 390	3673	TRUE 1066 FALSE 2607
R = S/C	2607	MIN=9.99191492E-01 MAX= 9.99136006E-01
D(I+1) = S*E(I) + C*D(I+1)	2607	MIN=1.20733366E-01 MAX= 1.20000066E-01
P = E(I+1) = R	2607	MIN=2.48714049E-01 MAX= 2.48709748E-01
S = C*E(I+1)	2607	MIN=1.24430618E-01 MAX= 1.25720006E-01
ASSIGN 340 TO RETURN	2607	
GO TO 900	2607	BRANCH 1 2607
340 E(I) = R*NORM	2607	MIN=1.01000576E-01 MAX= 1.10019000E-01
E(I+1) = 0	2607	MIN=1.24536618E-01 MAX= 1.17526898E-01
GO TO 380	2607	BRANCH 1 2607
390 S = C*E(I+1) + S*D(I+1)	1066	MIN=1.29093016E-01 MAX= 1.04401016E-01
Q = S*E(I+1)	1066	MIN=6.72043676E-02 MAX= 6.02773336E-01
D(I+1) = C*P/S + W	1066	MIN=1.15093396E-01 MAX= 1.23033196E-01
E(I+1) = C*E(I+1)	1066	MIN=9.10444936E-02 MAX= 4.42649926E-02
ASSIGN 360 TO RETURN	1066	
GO TO 900	1066	BRANCH 1 1066
360 E(I) = NORM	1066	MIN= 9.99716090E-01 MAX= 4.92000000E-01
380 CONTINUE	3793	
TEMP = C*E(NUM1) + S*D(NU)	117	MIN=1.56024256E-03 MAX= 3.14366126E-03
D(NU) = -S*E(NUM1) + C*D(NU)	117	MIN=1.20234008E-01 MAX= 1.20060006E-01
E(NUM1) = TEMP	117	MIN=1.56024256E-03 MAX= 3.14366126E-03
C		
C INTERNAL PROCEDURE TO CALCULATE THE ROTATION CORRESPONDING TO		
C THE VECTOR(P,Q).		
C		
900 TO 910	117	BRANCH 1 117
900 PP =ABS(P)	3790	MIN=1.28377638E-05 MAX= 9.42330038E-01
QQ =ABS(Q)	3790	MIN= 1.34028338E-13 MAX= 4.21300520E-01
IF(PP .GT. QQ) GO TO 910 QQ MUST >ZERO	3790	TRUE 1071 FALSE 2719
NORM = PP*SQRT(1.0 + (QQ/PP)**2)	2719	MIN= 4.30493395E-04 MAX= 4.42530638E-01
GO TO 920	2719	BRANCH 1 2719
910 IF(QQ .EQ. 0.0) GO TO 930 HENCE, NEVER TRUE	1071	TRUE 0 FALSE 1071
NORM = QQ*SQRT(1.0 + (PP/QQ)**2)	1071	MIN=1.68461265E-03 MAX= 4.21300520E-01
920 C = P/NORM	3790	MIN=1.00000000E+00 MAX= 1.00300000E+00
S = Q/NORM	3790	MIN=1.00000000E+00 MAX= 6.09900000E-01
GO TO RETURN,(310,340,360)	3790	BRANCH 1 117 BRANCH 2 2607
		BRANCH 3 1066
930 C = 1.0		
S = 0.0 IMPOSSIBLE TO REACH AS IS	:	:
NORM = 0.0	:	:
C		
C FIND REMAINING EIGENVECTORS (IF ANY) BY INVERSE ITERATION.		
C		
C		
C IF ALL EIGENVALUES WERE OBTAINED (FAIL = 0), THEN ALL EIGENVECTORS		
C WERE EITHER COMPUTED ALREADY BY ROTATION OR THE REMAINING EIGENVECTORS		
C NOT OBTAINED BY INVERSE ITERATION (LIMIT = 0). IF ALL EIGENVALUES		
C WERE NOT OBTAINED (FAIL .NE. 0), STORE ERROR FLAG IN		
C ROT(1),...,ROT(FAIL), WHICH INDICATES THERE WILL BE NO EIGENVECTORS		
C FOR THE EIGENVALUES NOT FOUND. ALSO, ZERO OUT REMAINING LOCATIONS		
C OF ROT ARRAY. SEE COMMENT FOLLOWING STATEMENT NUMBER 627.		

Fig 58b. Sample PET Program Output. Source: STUCKI-IEEE-73.

116

PROGRAM EVALUATOR AND TESTER REPORT FOR PROGRAM AB33A

SYNTACTIC PROFILE

TOTAL NUMBER OF SOURCE STATEMENTS   1246

TYPE OF STATEMENT	NUMBER	PERCENT OF TOTAL
EXECUTABLE SOURCE	792	63.6
NONEXECUTABLE SOURCE	168	13.5
COMMENT	286	23.0
NONSTANDARD	10	0.8
BRANCH	274	N/A
CALL	24	N/A
UNFORMATTED I/O	0	N/A
FORMATTED I/O	61	N/A

OPERATIONAL PROFILE

TOTAL EXECUTION COUNT   1889544

TYPE OF STATEMENT	NO.EXECUTED	PERCENT EXECUTED
EXECUTABLE SOURCE	288	36.4
BRANCH	77	28.1
CALL	14	58.3
UNFORMATTED I/O	0	100.0
FORMATTED I/O	3	4.9

Figure 58 c. Program Summary Report. Source: STUCKI-IEEE-73.

PROGRAM EVALUATOR AND TESTER REPORT SUBROUTINE OPERATIONAL SUMMARY

SUBROUTINE NAME	NO. OF STATEMENTS EXECUTED	PERCENT EXECUTED	NO. OF CALLS EXECUTED	PERCENT EXECUTED	NO. OF BRANCHES EXECUTED	PERCENT EXECUTED
AB33	4	80.0	2	100.0	0	100.0
AB33A	36	94.7	8	88.9	5	71.4
ATTERR	8	50.0	0	0.0	2	40.0
ATTREF	46	71.9	2	100.0	14	53.8
CMG	159	49.5	2	33.3	47	27.8
CROSS	4	100.0	0	100.0	0	100.0
CRPROD	4	100.0	0	100.0	0	100.0
ERCOND	15	29.4	0	100.0	9	24.3
ERNOTE	1	50.0	0	100.0	0	100.0
EULER	11	100.0	0	100.0	0	100.0
PROGRAM	288	36.4	14	58.3	77	28.1

SUBROUTINES NOT EXECUTED

BBEND
BBINPT
CMARTY
DESAT
DOCK

Fig 58 d. Sample Module Summary Report. Source: STUCKI-IEEE-73.

```
TOTAL EXECUTION TIME FOR THIS CASE      157.814 SEC

TOTAL TIME IN MONITORED ROUTINES        108.010 SEC

TOTAL TIME IN OTHER ROUTINES             49.804 SEC
```

DETAILED SUBROUTINE TIME MONITORING

SUBROUTINE NAME	TIME RELATIVE TO MAXIMUM SUBROUTINE EXECUTION TIME (• = TWO PERCENT)	ACTUAL TIME IN SECONDS	PERCENT OF TOTAL MONITORED TIME
AB33		0.011	0.01
AB33A		0.071	0.07
ATTERR	• • • •	5.207	4.82
ATTREF	• • • • • • • • • • • • •	21.170	19.60
CMG	• •	73.960	68.48
CROSS	• • •	3.716	3.44
CRPROD	• • •	3.847	3.56
ERCOND		0.003	0.00
ERNOTE		0.019	0.02
EULER		0.006	0.01

```
TOTAL TIME IN POSTPROCESSOR               7.245 SEC
```

Fig 58e. Sample Module Timing Summary. Source: STUCKI-IEEE-73.

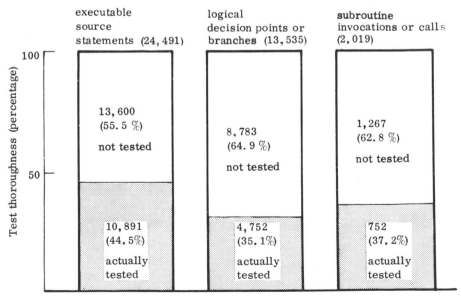

Fig 58f. Test Effectiveness Statistics (Sample Size 40,869 Source Statements). Source: STUCKI-750612 (Mc Donnell Douglas Automation).

SOURCE STATEMENT PROFILE:

Total Number of Source Statements in the Sample	40,869	
Number of Comment Statements	12,193	(29.8 %)
Number of Other Non-executable Statements (e.g., declaratives, type statements, etc.)	4,185	(10.2 %)
Number of Executable Statements	24,491	(59.9 %)

OTHER SOURCE STATEMENT MEASUREMENTS:

Number of Source State-ments Containing Coding Standards Violations	519	(1.3 %)
Number of Branches Con-tained in the Source Code	13,535	
Number of Subroutine Invocation Points (CALL statements in FORTRAN)	2,019	

Fig. 58g. PET SOURCE STATEMENT STATISTICS
Source: STUCKI-IEEE-73

ANNOTATED PROGRAM LISTING	EXECUTION COUNT	SPECIFIC EXECUTION DATA

102 K = K + 1	511	ASSERTION VIOLATIONS 1
		ASSERT RANGE (I,J,K,L)(0,100)
		    EXEC NUMBER VALUE
		        10 101

103 II = A(L,J) + LL	511	ASSERTION VIOLATIONS 3
		ASSERT RANGE (II,LL)(-10,10)
		    EXEC NUMBER VALUE
		        22 20
		ASSERT SUBSCRIPT RANGE(A(*,3))
		    EXEC NUMBER VALUE
		         5 A(12,3)
		       105 A(1,4)

234 K = A(J,K) + I*100	125	ASSERTION VIOLATIONS 4
		ASSERT RANGE (I,J,K,L)(0,100)
		    EXEC NUMBER VALUE
		        52 101
		        53 102
		ASSERT SUBSCRIPT RANGE (A(*,3))
		    EXEC NUMBER VALUE
		        52 A(5,4)
		        53 A(6,4)

235 II = II + 2	125	ASSERTION VIOLATIONS 1
		ASSERT RANGE (II,LL)(-10,10)
		    EXEC NUMBER VALUE
		        50 12

236 NN = KK*(I-J)	38	ASSERTION VIOLATIONS 1
		ASSERT VALUES (KK,NN)(2,4,6,8,10)
		    EXEC NUMBER VALUE
		        20 7

300 CALL ROUTINEX(X,Y)	53	ASSERTION VIOLATIONS 1
		ASSERT NO SIDE EFFECTS (X,Y,Z)
		                    VALUE OF CALL PARM X
		EXEC NUMBER BEFORE CALL AFTER CALL
		    30 -10 -20

Fig. 58 h. An example of the assertion violation automatic measurement
development in the PET software. Source: STUCKI-750421.

Program	AB33	AD77	F999	JOYCE	META	MI01	PTT	UT03	TOTALS
Total Number of Statements	1,578	11,111	2,833	3,033	1,125	775	772	1,445	22,672
No. of Comment Statements	355	3,847	644	176	86	189	44	54	5,395
Percentage of Total	22.5	34.6	22.7	5.8	7.6	24.4	5.7	3.7	23.8
No. Other Nonexecutable Statements	177	905	257	372	534	40	249	254	2,788
Percentage of Total	11.2	8.1	9.1	12.3	47.5	5.2	32.3	17.6	12.3
No. Standard's Violations	9	33	28	65	1	1	23	44	204
Percentage of Total	0.6	0.3	1.0	2.1	0.1	0.1	3.0	3.0	1.0
No. Executable Statements	1,046	6,359	1,932	2,485	505	546	479	1,137	14,489
Percentage of Total	66.3	57.2	68.2	81.9	44.9	70.5	62.0	78.7	63.9
No. Actually Executed	678	2,213	1,155	846	419	392	364	584	6,651
Percentage Executed	64.8	34.8	59.8	34.0	83.0	71.8	76.0	51.4	45.9
No. of Branches	357	2,635	859	1,718	355	189	333	510	6,956
Ave./Exec. Statements	0.34	0.41	0.44	0.69	0.70	0.35	0.70	0.45	0.48
No. Actually Executed	195	571	376	454	203	112	175	175	2,261
Percentage Executed	54.6	21.7	43.8	26.4	57.2	59.3	52.6	34.3	32.5
No. of CALL Statements	20	369	86	278	32	9	19	99	912
Ave./Exec. Statements	0.02	0.06	0.04	0.11	0.06	0.02	0.04	0.09	0.06
No. Actually Executed	18	119	26	67	21	3	5	76	335
Percentage Executed	90.0	32.2	30.2	24.1	65.6	33.3	26.3	76.8	36.7
Total Statement Exec. Counts (in thousands)	26,772	2,929	112	1,129	5,284	1,133	1,087	71	38,517

Fig 58i. Actual Program Statistics with the Program Testing Translator. Source: STUCKI-7208.

Automatic measurement of program code adherance to standards at TRW

In Fig 50 a program called "CODE AUDITOR" is listed. This program reads FORTRAN source programs and checks adherance to standards, much as a human code inspector might do in Fagan's I-2, discussed earlier.

As examples of the restrictions that this program checks for, TRW gives:

1. Comment to precede statement labels (all labels must be commented)
       C BEGINNING OF XYZ CALCULATION.
        123   A = 0
2. Common blocks to be labeled
3. No arguments on subroutine statements
    . . .
17. 100 executable statements maximum per routine
18. END preceded by executable statement other than a RETURN? (Error)

Fig 60 shows the detailed output from a CODE AUDITOR run on a FORTRAN source program. Ninety-five percent ($1.00 - \frac{314}{6275}$) of the statements are in accordance with standards. It is "95% standard". We have a measuring instrument for the degree of standardization of source code according to installation standard (not to be confused with ANSI or ISO language standards).

A summary of the number of violations of each type of standard is given for each routine.

Fig 59 shows results of a large part of the same software system ("Site Defense" software at an early stage). The 89% accordance with standards was considered good at that point in development. Obviously the "PCP" group need to be reminded about standards.

- PERFORMANCE INDEX $= \dfrac{\text{NO. OF DISCREPANCIES}}{\text{NO. OF CARD IMAGES}}$

- TAP $\qquad \dfrac{317}{6275} = 5\%$

- SETS/RTP $\qquad \dfrac{351}{4747} = 7\%$

- SETS/OGP $\qquad \dfrac{2448}{21,203} = 11\%$

- PCP $\qquad \dfrac{3974}{30,207} = 13\%$

TOTAL $\qquad \dfrac{7090}{62,432} = 11\%$

FORTRAN SOURCE CODE

Fig 59. CODE AUDITOR PERFORMANCE INDEX

$$\text{PERFORMANCE INDEX} = \frac{\text{NUMBER OF DISCREPANCIES}}{\text{TOTAL NUMBER OF CARD IMAGES}} = \frac{314}{6275} = 0.05$$

ROUTINE NAME			STANDARD NUMBER			TOTAL
	1	2	3 17	18		
TTARS	2	0	0 . . 0	0		26
TTILT	15	0	0 . . 1	0		17

Fig 60. ERROR SUMMARY REPORT

Automatic judgement of program "readability"

The Datalogical Institute at the University of Copenhagen has conducted experiments to see what correlation exists between human judgement of program readability and automatic judgement, using a program to read another source program (Report 75/1 in Danish). It is called "PLIX", a program readability index. The scale of judgement was from 1 (very easy to read) to 7 (very difficult). Forty-eight ALGOL programs, comprising 304 pages of 66 lines of code, were examined.

An English translation of this report, and further research reports combining PLIX and Weissman's experiments, are expected in 1976 and are listed here in the references under Andersen.

Measurement of data base quality by automated inspection

Data bases, or any other large and complex machine-readable collections of data, need automated tools for measuring their quality (see Fig 61). If these tools are not designed and built into the total system, then there is a risk that the necessary control fields in the data base records will not have been designed into each record in the data base. As a result, automated diagnosis will become inefficient and ineffective.

A list of control fields which need to be present in each data base record in order to facilitate automatic measurement of data base quality are indicated in Fig 63. Fields 4, 5, 8, 9 and 12 are directly used as measuring tools and the other fields are used to select appropriate subsets of the data base for measurement.

Fig 64 contains a list of the basic design concepts for a data base diagnosis program. One large Australian bank which implemented such a tool on my advice for a one million account on line file that had been operating "successfully" for eight years, reported some months later that the first run of the diagnosis program produced a list of 300,000 errors which had to be corrected. Most of these were discovered by relational checks between related records and fields. Most of the errors were in the statistical/marketing categories of the account holders. This had led to top management reports containing serious inaccuracies for many years. Management was extremely disturbed by this revelation of the inaccuracy of their data base. The cause of the errors seems to be largely due to the use of abstract numeric codes (01 = steelworker, 02 = housewife, etc.), which were never checked once they had passed table lookup type validity checks. Management decreed that data base diagnosis

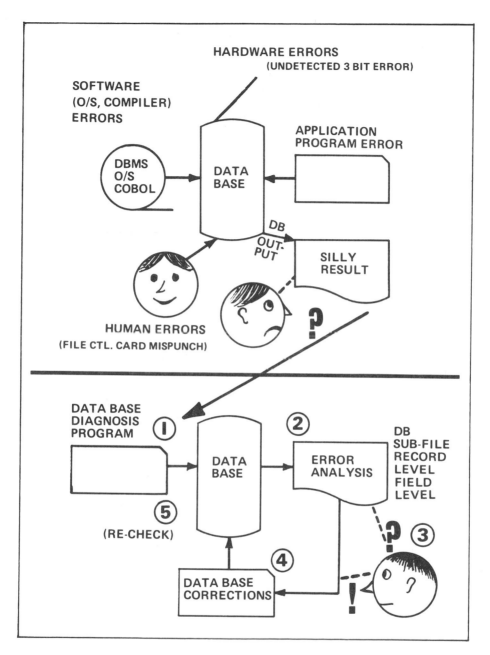

Fig 61. AUTOMATIC ERROR DIAGNOSIS

```
EXAMPLE OF DATA BASE DIAGNOSIS CONTROL FUNCTIONS


. DIAG

. DATE 75 MAY 8 ,  75 MAY 12

. TYPE CUST ,  EMPL

. REPORT TOTALS, 1. LINE,  PAGE

. LIMIT-OUT  10 PAGES

. LIMIT-IN   500 CASES

. FROM HAAK ,  10030

. SAMPLE  10 ,  RAND

. TEST RLHT
```

Fig 62.

was to be run once a day, every day. The daily machine time involved
was said to be 20 minutes.

Last time I had contact with them, all the branch offices were feverishly
correcting the 300, 000 errors.

Data bases are the "dataware" part of software, and the programs that
make use of incorrect data bases may themselves produce unreliable
results. It is unrealistic to expect the application programs to make all
possible validity checks before using data. In any case database diagnosis
provides early detection or measurement of problems, so they can be
corrected before use.

CONTROL FIELDS IN DATABASE RECORD DESIGNS WHICH YOU MIGHT
CONSIDER

CONTROL FIELDS /	APPLICATION DATA FIELDS
EXAMPLE ⌄	TYPE OF FIELD ⌄
CUST	1. RECORD TYPE
23456	2. UNIQUE IDENTIFIER (within record type)
JOHN	3. CHECK WORD AND ALPHABETIC SORT KEY
740520	4. CHANGE STAMP: THE UPDATING PROGRAM NAME, TRANSACTION NUMBER, DATA AND TIME OF UPDATE
????	5. HEALTH INDICATOR (sick, suspicious, OK)
120354	6. POINTER (primary chain of records) MAIN SEQUENCE
120350	7. POINTER (secondary chain, related records = variable length)
10110001	8. RECORD LEVEL HASH TOTAL FOR CONTROL FIELDS
11101101	9. RECORD LEVEL HASH TOTAL FOR APPLICATION DATA
0	10. SECURITY CLASSIFICATION (right to modify, to read)
TSG	11. SECURITY: LAST TERMINAL OR USER TO ACCESS OR MODIFY
2	12. ACTIVITY COUNT: FOR SECURITY (unusual activity) OR FOR OPTIMIZATION INSTRUMEN-TATION OF RECORD
TSG	13. INTERLOCK: A SIGNAL THAT THE RECORD IS PRESENTLY BEING UPDATED OR MAY BE MODIFIED BY OTHERS (code for terminal or user)
	14. RESERVED FOR FUTURE ADDITIONS

Fig 63. Source: GILB, DATA ENGINEERING.

- POST THE DATE AND TIME OF CURRENT DIAGNOSIS IN DB-CONTROL RECORD

- POST SUMMARY RESULTS OF DIFFERENT ERROR CHECKS IN DB-CONTROL RECORD (and use this information to allow other programs to judge health)

- REPEAT ALL POSSIBLE LOGICAL CHECKS WHICH YOU HAVE MADE IN OTHER PROGRAMS

- CHECK CORRELATION BETWEEN INDEXES AND RECORDS

- CHECK POINTERS/CHAINS/LINKAGES BETWEEN RECORDS

- MAP OUT AND ACCOUNT FOR APPARENTLY "UNUSED" SPACE: CHECK CONTENTS

- EXTENSIVE RECORD RELATIONSHIP CONTROL (supplier of the part: example)

- DESIGN PROGRAM TO GIVE RESULTS IN DIFFERENT "DETECTION LEVELS"

- DESIGN PROGRAM IN HIGHLY GENERALIZED MANNER: ALLOW USER CONTROL OF EXTENT, DEPTH OF ANALYSIS, TYPE OF CHECK, OUTPUT FORMAT AND EXTENT

- DESIGN PROGRAM FOR EXTENSION AS EXPERIENCE INDICATES

- HUMANIZE THE PARAMETERS IN THE PROGRAM CONTROL LANGUAGE

- RUN AS LOW PRIORITY JOB IN OTHERWISE UNUSED COMPUTER TIME FOR CONSTANT HEALTH DIAGNOSIS AND EARLY WARNING OF PROBLEMS

- DESIGN WITH RANDOM SAMPLING OF RECORDS AND TEST DEPTH

Fig 64. AUTO $\frac{\text{FILE}}{\text{DB}}$ HEALTH DIAGNOSIS TECHNIQUES

PART II

Metric concepts

Introduction to Part II

This section contains a set of basic software metrics and suggested definitions, together with illustrative material.

It cannot pretend to be complete. As other disciplines have demonstrated, each application requires its own concepts and tools for measuring the essential properties of the system concerned.

It can, however, give the reader a basic set of concepts upon which to build when devising additional measuring tools. Hopefully, some of these concepts will stand the test of time and usefulness and will become part of our common communication system about our technology.

At the very least, the student of this technology cannot complain that there is no measuring concept for a particular quality.

The role of metrics concepts in the software design process

In Fig 65 the step "System Attribute Specification" can make direct use of the metric concepts suggested here.

The following detailed technical design steps, 1 to 5, should constantly make use of the attribute metrics in order to determine whether or not the techniques being considered can provide the set of attributes demanded in the system attribute specification.

Metrics is the language we can use for precise matching of available techniques to the user's requirements.

Influence of metrics on many levels of our technology

Metrics can be applied to many different levels of description of systems and the techniques that are used to construct those systems.

The same metric concepts can be used to specify what we want, to predict what we can expect to get, and to measure what we have gotten.

"PROGRAM" DESIGN

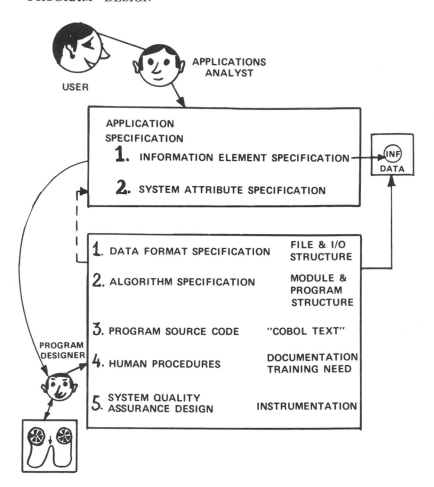

USER

APPLICATIONS ANALYST

APPLICATION SPECIFICATION

1. INFORMATION ELEMENT SPECIFICATION

2. SYSTEM ATTRIBUTE SPECIFICATION

INF DATA

1. DATA FORMAT SPECIFICATION   FILE & I/O STRUCTURE

2. ALGORITHM SPECIFICATION   MODULE & PROGRAM STRUCTURE

3. PROGRAM SOURCE CODE   "COBOL TEXT"

4. HUMAN PROCEDURES   DOCUMENTATION TRAINING NEED

5. SYSTEM QUALITY ASSURANCE DESIGN   INSTRUMENTATION

PROGRAM DESIGNER

Fig 65. Step 2 "System Attribute Specification" is carried out with the help of metric concepts, and is a critical step to the structural design work in the next five design areas.

Metrics provides us with a powerful language for describing the relation-ships which we desire, expect or experience in any group of subsystems.

The metrics language is independent of the functional process or structure of any particular system part. It tells us about the quality of the subsystem without forcing us to describe the functional details which give rise to the metrically described qualities.

Metrics allows us to concentrate on the final end-requirements of the users for whom we construct systems, without burdening them or us (too early, at least) with the functional details of the systems.

Since metrics is a neutral language, describing goals and not particular techniques which might satisfy those goals, it is a highly suitable tool for a rapidly changing technology. See Fig 66.

In a stable technology (over many generations for example) we speak and think mostly in terms of the techniques, because they have well-known attributes and we do not expect to see these techniques displaced by more powerful ones, nor do we expect radically new needs to be demanded of us by the users.

In a rapidly changing technology we must expect to search for and find new (for us at least) technological devices to satisfy new and increased demands on our systems by the users. Metrics allows us to describe systems composed of any set of qualities, even those that seem beyond our present capabilities. Once described, we have a tool for searching for adequate technology to satisfy the high requirements demanded of us, or at the very least we can assert that we do not know, at present, how to build systems for that set of qualities. We have thus defined the frontier, the state of our art, and this challenges the inventive and imaginative or the ambitious to push forward. This motivation to improve technology systematically usually results in a common improvement, for all of us, in the state of our art.

Multidimensional system description

Fig 67 shows one way of imagining the multidimensional quality description of a system and its related subsystems.

Initially, the system can be described by means of the major quality borderlines for the system as a whole. For example:

- its minimum and expected reliability

- the minimum maintainability

- (or at a higher level the availability describes both the above)

- its cost (in implementation, operation and maintenance)

- its implementation time and effort

- its work capacity and speed-of-response.

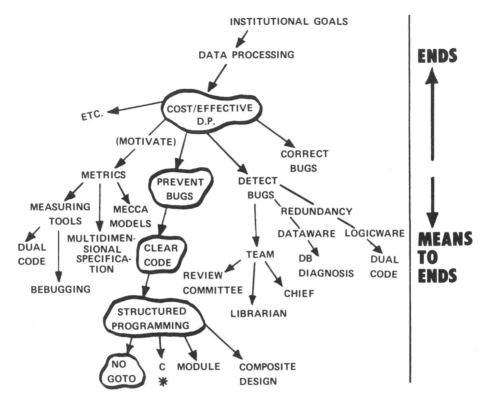

Fig 66. Many roads lead to Rome. Each of the roads shown here has a cost and a value for a particular user. Many of these roads must be used at the same time.

In addition to this basic description, metrics can be used to some extent to describe variations from desired or expected values of system quality (indicated by the dotted lines in the figure).

We can discuss the possible alternatives, the ideal, or the limits of the quality.

Then we can break the system into sublevels, in order to analyze the different elements that contribute to the whole system. We may be interested in making divisions so as to progress with more detailed design work. This enables us to see more clearly the metric values that each subsystem must contribute in order for the overall system to have the qualities expected of it.

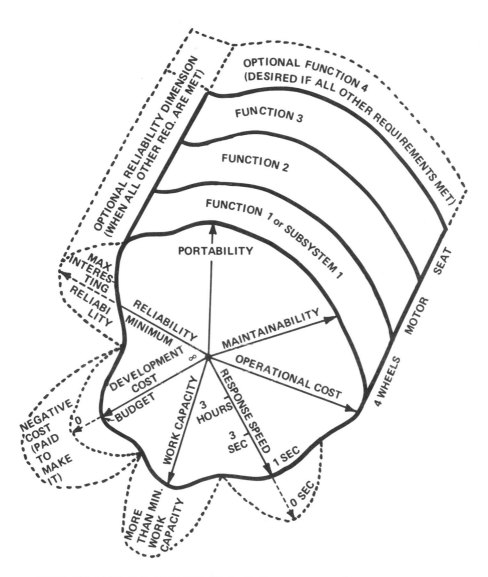

REQUIREMENT/PROPERTIES MATRIX
OR
SUBSYSTEM and QUALITY
(OF SUBSYSTEM) RELATIONSHIP

Fig 67.

135

We may be interested in dividing up an existing system in order to look for weak points which are capable of easy improvement ("value analysis").

The process of hierarchical description and analysis is well known and appreciated. The use of metrics to describe the resulting system components and their relationship to each other improves this process substantially.

System design goals and constraints

Some of the main specifications regarding the reliability, cost and adaptability of a system are shown in Fig 68.

The first area of trade-off between desirable qualities and the cost of designing these qualities into the system is indicated in the top rectangles INITIAL RESOURCE INVESTMENT and SYSTEM EFFECTIVENESS.

In most real systems there is no question of perfection, but simply of getting satisfactory system effectiveness at an acceptable cost. The use of metrics to describe these relationships will tend to give the system designer a better basis for making predictions and better control over the results.

Another area of trade-off is between the short-term effectiveness of the system and its long-term effectiveness in the form of survival in the face of changing requirements. The priority given to either of these development goals depends on the application at hand and the decision must be made with reference to a particular application and to the subjective priorities of those responsible for the project.

The MECCA method, discussed earlier, is a practical tool for representing such a hierarchy of goals and for including the relative priority assigned to each goal by the evaluator and the alternative designs, bids, techniques or technologies which are offered for satisfying these goals.

Dataware metrics

In any single subsystem, for any particular user of that system, there is a particular set of goals and subgoals which have the greatest relevance for that user.

DESIGN SPECIFICATION RELATIONSHIPS

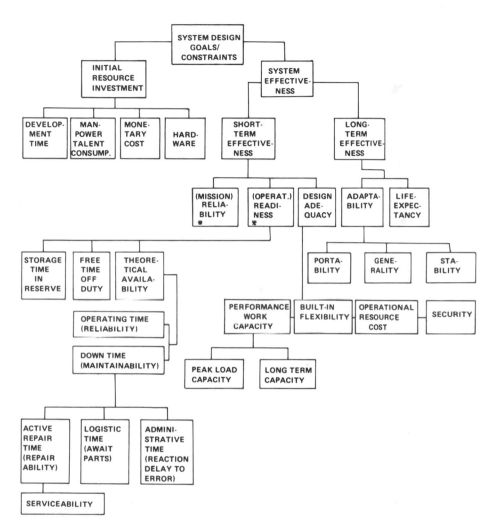

* (ARINC Res. Corp., Welker in Reliability Handbook)

Copyright 1972 Gilb

Fig 68.

137

DATAWARE ATTRIBUTES

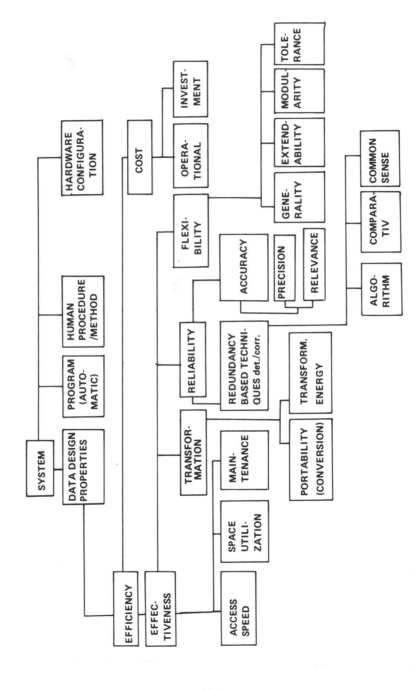

Fig 69. Some selected data concepts. Simplified relationships in terms of design goals/constraints.

These, naturally, will be included in the specifications and descriptions of the system by the user. The other properties of the system will continue to exist, in spite of not being described.

For example, when describing dataware subsystems (input codes, record designs or perhaps data bases, for example) the metrics in Fig 69 could be useful to describe the _properties_ of that design, dataware technique or data subsystem.

All of these metrics can be related to their contribution to other subsystems, and to higher-level goals. None of them are entirely isolated from the highest level goals of the system.

Again, in order to remind the reader-technologist that the whole design exercise in the real world must consider the initial development costs and the ongoing operational costs, I have specifically included the concept of cost, which is intended in the broadest sense of the term: not only money but people and time.

Data base multidimensional properties

Fig 70 shows that a data base, this complex but critical and central subsystem of a data processing system, can be described by means of the metrics described in the following pages.

These metrics can be used to specify desired properties, to evaluate alternative designs and software packages for data base support, and, finally, to judge the data base as a unit apart from the programs which access it, in terms of its current quality.

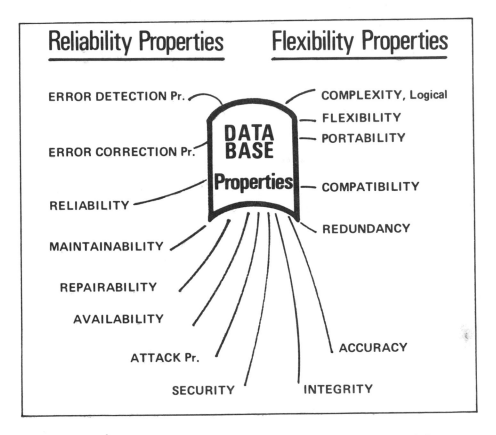

Fig 70. Data bases and other files can be described by means of the same attributes used to describe other software, such as programs.

Reliability metrics

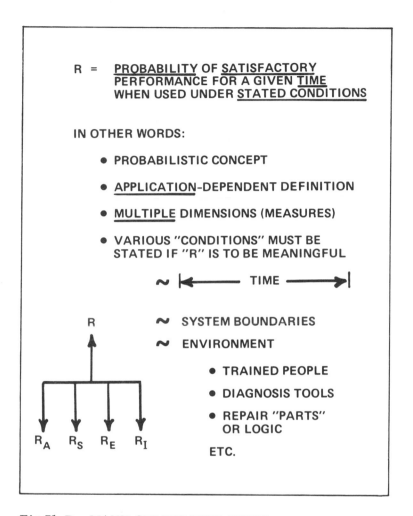

R = PROBABILITY OF SATISFACTORY PERFORMANCE FOR A GIVEN TIME WHEN USED UNDER STATED CONDITIONS

IN OTHER WORDS:

- PROBABILISTIC CONCEPT
- APPLICATION-DEPENDENT DEFINITION
- MULTIPLE DIMENSIONS (MEASURES)
- VARIOUS "CONDITIONS" MUST BE STATED IF "R" IS TO BE MEANINGFUL

~ TIME

~ SYSTEM BOUNDARIES

~ ENVIRONMENT

- TRAINED PEOPLE
- DIAGNOSIS TOOLS
- REPAIR "PARTS" OR LOGIC

ETC.

R — R_A R_S R_E R_I

Fig 71. R = MANY-SPLENDORED THING

Reliability of any system

Metric

Pr. $R_s(t)$ = reliability probability of system s during time t

Reliability is the probability that the system will perform satisfactorily (with no malfunctions) for at least a given time interval, when used under stated conditions.

In practice, the concept of reliability is heavily dependent on subjective and application-dependent judgements as to the concepts of "satisfactory performance" and "malfunctions".

These must be clearly defined, if the measure is to be meaningful.

Reliability is typically dependent on, and composed of, other concepts (see Fig 72) such as:

1. actual operating time (non-failed state, active)

2. down time (in a failed state, needs repair), which is dependent on maintainability factors
   a. active repair time (debug, correct, analyze)
   b. logistic time (awaiting listings, manuals)
   c. administrative time (calling in systems programmers, etc.)

Example: $R_{O/S}$ (24 hours) = .9100 means that the Operating/System is expected to function correctly for 24 hours, 91% of the days, and to have at least one breakdown 9% of the days in operation.

Reliability - concept comments

Definition: consistency of a quality, for example performance.

Notes:

a. The concept of system reliability is relative to the system quality being measured.

   Thus there may be as many reliability measures for a system as there are qualities to be measured. Consequently we would normally indicate which quality we are measuring the consistency of when we give a reliability figure. For example we can distinguish between pure functional reliability (Is it functioning at all or is it "down"?) and effectiveness (Is it consistently producing the effect on its environment which it was designed to produce?).

b. "Probability" is a widely recognized measuring concept for reliability.

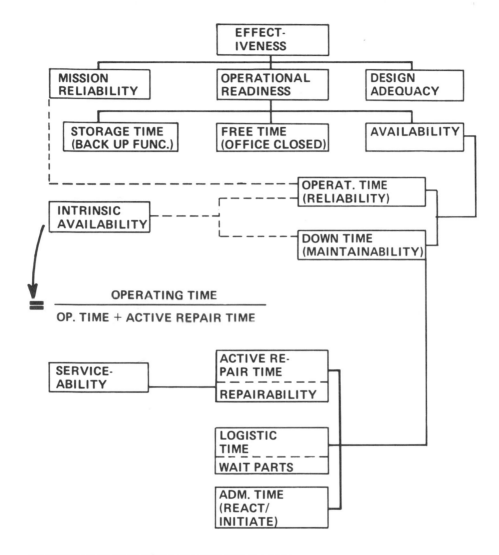

BEAUTY IS IN THE EYES OF THE BEHOLDER

Fig 72. Source: Reliability Handbook, McGraw-Hill.

c. "Perfect reliability" (100% probability of successful system operation under the conditions of intended use) of any system may be considered unobtainable in the long run, or at best "infinitely costly" and thus of no practical interest.

d. In general it can be observed in any system that the incremental cost of reliability increases very sharply (as it turns towards infinity) at the higher end of the scale (in the 90% and over range).

e. This means that it is critical to system cost that we have control over the degree of reliability being designed and constructed into the system.

   We must select a satisfactory degree of reliability and avoid any unrewarding effort or costs towards a higher degree of reliability.

f. On the other hand, if we fix the costs, resources or time available for a system and we do not exercise similar control over reliability, then it is likely to become the "variable factor" or uncontrollable variable. It is likely that reliability will suffer in the initial implementation, only to have to be corrected to a satisfactory level by additional time, resources and money effort.

g. Functional reliability (Is it working or not?) can be applied to a system or any one of its components (subsystems).

   The functional reliability of a system is directly dependent on the functional reliability of its components as well as their relationship to one another. Knowing the reliability and relationship of components will allow us to calculate total system reliability. (See RAU-1970.)

h. Other reliability measures ("effectiveness" measures) may not have any calculable relationship to other system components since each component's "effectiveness" is defined by its particular mission alone in its environment.

i. When there is, at the system level, some common measurable purpose (example: error detection) then it is possible to apply calculation techniques like those used in fuctional reliability calculations. For details of reliability calculation see for example RAU, IRESON, and MACHOL.

Reliability of a computer program

Metric

A computer program is also a system, so the previous definition applies (Pr. R(t)).

However, this section contains some specific details of the definition of a program reliability measure.

Program reliability (or "logicware" reliability) is defined as the probability that a given (software) program operates for a certain time period, without a logical error, on the machine for which it was designed, provided it is used within the design limits.

Software errors are defined as deficiencies in fidelity, veracity, or viability, as follows:

a. Fidelity is defined as the accuracy with which a given algorithm is mechanized for a given operating system and hardware system.

b. Veracity is defined as the adequacy with which a given algorithm represents the requirements of the physical world.

c. Viability is defined as the adequacy with which a given algorithm meets timing constraints.

More detailed mathematics and experimental data on this subject will be found in the source of the above definitions: DICKSON-1972.

Reliability of a program or "logicware reliability" - Concept Comments

Just as "hardware" logical systems can have both "solid" and "intermittent" failures, so can software systems.

A "solid" software failure may result in program abortion ("ABEND") and may or may not have automatic analysis and recovery procedures. Intermittent software failures will result from certain combinations of logic and data. They may only result in "non-productivity" (an error message instead of a productive result). The system may automatically "recover" and continue executing the program and looking at new data, without human intervention or intervention of error recovery procedures.

In a data base-oriented system, the unreliable state may have produced invalid results on a magnetic storage medium which are not immediately discoverable, but which will cause system trouble later on.

A pragmatic measure. A TRW-Systems publication defined program reliability as:

$$1 - \frac{\text{number of inputs with execution failures}}{\text{total number of inputs}}$$

(pp. 5-22 of TRW-SS-74-14).

Maintainability

Pr. M_s (t) = the probability that, when maintenance action is initiated under stated conditions, a failed system (s) will be restored to operable condition within a specified time (t).

Maintainability is a function of such primary factors as:

a. design of the system: diagnostic aids, documentation, built-in diagnostic aids, automatic recovery procedures.

b. personnel: especially their skill level (experience, training, intelligence, motivation)

c. support facilities: locally available tools and diagnostic test equipment or aids, spare parts/alternative program versions/back-up files, the organization responsible.

(Adapted with modifications from Ross H. D, "Reliability" in Machol (ed.) System Engineering Handbook, pp. 33-14, McGraw-Hill 1965.)

Repairability

Pr. Repairability_s (t) = the probability that a failed system (s) will be restored to operable condition within a specified active repair time (t), when maintenance is done under specified conditions.

This differs from the higher-level concept of maintainability in that such

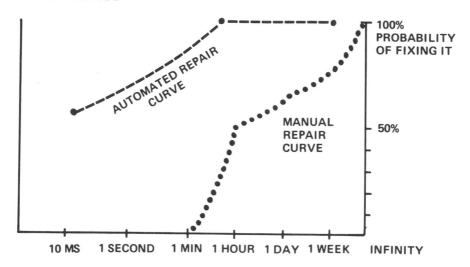

Fig 73. Software can be repaired automatically using the same principles
of redundancy planning that hardware systems use for automatic
repair. For programs, a simple example of bug repair is based
on the dual-but-distinct program-module concept, discussed
elsewhere in this text. Dataware repair is based on sufficient
data redundancy's being initially planned into the system, with
suitable logicware to detect the error and decide on a suitable
repair (Source: Gilb, Teaching Aids Collection, 1975)

waiting time factors such as tools (diagnostic programs), parts (backup copies of files, etc.) and people, are assumed to be immediately
present. In other words, repairability depends more on the nature of
the object to be repaired than on the factors leading up to the active
repair phase. In a sense it is a measure of the "inherent maintainability",
to which must be added delays due to calling in qualified technicians,
spare modules or data copies, etc.

Serviceability is the degree of ease or difficulty with which a system
can be repaired. It is reflected in such factors as repairability, but it
is not considered directly quantifiable at present (see Welker, "System
Effectiveness" pp. 1-7 in Ireson (ed.) Reliability Handbook, McGraw-
Hill, 1966).

Check list

DESIGN of technology

- DATA STRUCTURES (limit error det./error corr./portability)
- LOGICAL STRUCTURE (algorithm), (dual code)
- DOCUMENTATION
- DIAGNOSTIC TOOLS
- RECOVERY SYSTEM DESIGN
- INSTRUMENTATION (measuring M by built-in logic)

PEOPLE as individuals

- SPECIALIZATION
- EXPERIENCE
- TRAINING
- INTELLIGENCE
- MOTIVATION

ORGANIZATION of people
to do maintenance

- GEOGRAPHICAL ACCESS TO PROBLEM (in California?)
- ALTERNATIVES (planned if main way fails)
- ORGANIZATION (communication, responsibility)
- MOTIVATION
- MEASURING PROCEDURES (accept test spec in contract?)

Fig 74. Maintainability in a real software system is affected by a wide
range of system design decisions. It cannot be the province of
"programmers" alone, since decisions about for example, fundamental data design, individual training and organizational reaction
ability, are involved. Source: Gilb, Teaching Aids, 1975.

SOME DESIGN ALTERNATIVES

- DESIGN INSPECTIONS (I_1, FAGAN of IBM)
- CODE INSPECTIONS (I_2)
- PEOPLE SELECTION (BY BEBUGGING TEST FOR EXAMPLE)
- READERS OF PROGRAMS ON TEAM (WEINBERG)
- AUTOMATED LIBRARIAN AUDIT OF COMMENTS (TRW)
- TEST PATH ANALYSIS PROGRAMS (GRC & RXVP & TRW)
- PSEUDO CODE DOCUMENTATION IS COMPUTER READABLE (APL)
- DUALLY MAINTAINED CODE GIVES TEST CASE PRODUCTION AND COMPARISON AUTOMATION
- MODULARIZATION (WHICH GROUPING, SIZE, INTERFACE)
- "STRUCTURED" PROGRAM LOGIC FLOW
- FILE DIAGNOSIS PROGRAM (FINDS SIDE EFFECTS OF NEW MAINTENANCE BUG)
- ADDITIONAL DATA—STRUCTURE REDUNDANCY (TO ALLOW PROGRAMS MORE PROBABILITY OF DETECTING/CORRECTING ERRORS)

Fig 75. Specific design techniques must be applied to improve the maintainability of software. Each technique should be measured both before it is applied (in terms of expected quantitative result in improving maintainability) and in the operational system (to verify that the expected result has been attained and is still present). Many of these techniques are discussed in the first part of this text.

Availability

Pr. A_s = the probability that a system (s) is operating satisfactorily at any point in time, when used under stated conditions.

= time actually available/time that should have been available.

149

Conventional reliability engineering uses the following definitions:

1. Intrinsic availability $Ai = \dfrac{\text{operate time}}{\text{operate time + active down time}}$

   or alternatively $\qquad Ai = \dfrac{\text{Mean Time To Maintenance (MTTM)}}{\text{MTTM + mean active down time}}$

2. Operational availability $Ao = \dfrac{\text{operate time}}{\text{operate time + \underline{total} down time}}$

   total down time = active down time + down time when the system
   was not actually needed
   but was turned on (ready).

3. Use availability $Au = \dfrac{\text{operate time + off-time}}{\text{operate time + off-time + total down time}}$

   thus including the concept of non-use (off) time.
   The difference is to account for systems which have a very large
   off-time compared to their total use.

A clear statement should accompany an availability value, showing
how it was calculated and with what intention it is used.

Examples of application areas: availability of particular application
files in an on-line state, availability of an on-line terminal, availability
of an on-line software executive.

(Source of definitions: Reliability Handbook, op. cit. pp. 11-10)

Attack probability

An attack on a system is any defined circumstance which results in a
given probability of error, failure, error detection, error correction,
security breach, etc.

Pr. At_s (a , t) = the probability of an attack of type a on system s
during time interval t.

This is an expression of the frequency with which latent problems occur.
The success of these latent problems is then determined by the effectiveness of the error detection, error correction and security devices which
are able to handle that type of attack.

Examples of types of attacks:

150

- sabotage

- invalid data values

- invalid combinations of valid data element values in input

- a program logic error

- attempt by an operator to mount an old generation of the "correct" file

- breakdown of computer's air-conditioning during a heat wave.

An alternative term, used in connection with system security technology, is "threat". Threat analysis looks at the potential attacks on a system.

Sensitivity (of information)

The sensitivity of stored information is a measure of its "cost of exposure" (Taylor, Eurocomp-74, p. 1008).

Taylor suggests a draft scale for the purpose of generating a risk measure for data bases. (Risk = size x sensitivity x accessibility.)

SCALE VALUE	EXAMPLE
10	Secret information at national level, diplomatic secrets, defense secrets.
9	Police records relating to convictions.
8	"Confidential" police records, of use to private enquiry agents. IQ test results.
7	Commercial data, relating to organizations. Trade or design secrets.
6	More sensitive financial information, company finances.
5	General financial information - bank records, medical records, payroll.
4	Vehicle licencing system, etc., which can be misused for criminal activities.
3	Educational pupil information in schools - related to personality & behavior.
2	Account enquiry systems - can be used for tracing defaulted debtors.
1	"Selected" general information (age, title/profession, address).
0	Constructive information. For example a list of doctors. Providing use related to purpose intended when contents gathered. Literature abstracts. Data banks of generally available engineering components.

Fig 76.

Taylor's "size" concept (mentioned above) is a linear projection on a logarithmic scale, where the maximum size is that of the total population of his country (55 million), which is assumed to be the largest data bank size. The largest size has a value of 10 on his scale.

See also "Accessibility" below.

SYSTEM INTEGRITY MEASURES

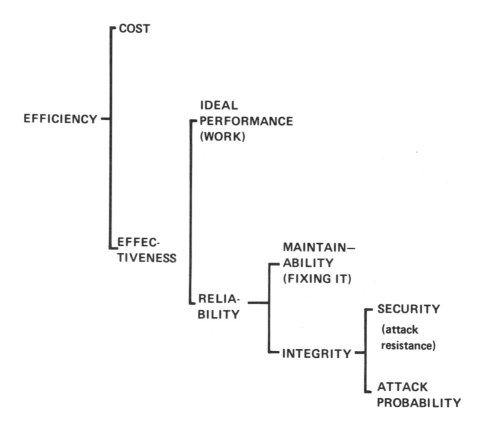

Fig 77.

Security probability: attack repulsion probability

Pr. $S_s(a)$ = the probability of successful attack (type a) rejection in system s, at any time.

152

This concept is very close to the concept of error detection probability and assumes something similar to "error correction", but not exactly so, in that the security attack is turned away and is not successful. It may be ignored, corrected or captured.

Integrity probability: system survival probability

$$\text{Pr. } Ig_s = 1 - [At \times (1-S)]$$

In other words, system survival is dependent on the frequency of system attack coupled with the ability of the system to make itself secure from a particular type of attack.

If all possible attacks on the system were a = 1, 2, 3, 4 ...n, the probability of survival from all attacks must be the product of all corresponding system integrity probabilities:

$$Ig_s (t) = \prod_{a=1}^{n} Ig_s (a, t)$$

The concepts of At, S, Ig have, as yet, no tradition. I propose them as a tool for more systematic evaluation of security system design. See GILB-READ-74 for the first published proposal of these concepts.

Accessibility (ease of access to a system)

This is a reflection of the probability of intentional and accidental breaking into a system. It is a security measure, and the term security could be used instead.

Taylor (EUROCOMP-74, Proceedings p. 1018, reference 19) proposes a draft scale for accessibility: Fig 79.

RESPONSIBILITY	SYMBOL	DEFINITION

Attack

SYSTEM ANALYST	$At_s\,(a, t)$	= PROBABILITY of ATTACK of TYPE "a", DURING TIME "t" FOR SYSTEM "s"

Security

SYSTEM DESIGNER	$S_s\,(a)$	= PROBABILITY of SUCCESSFULL RESISTANCE to ATTACK TYPE "a"

Integrity

FINAL SYSTEM CONTRACTOR or USER	$Ig_s\,(a, t)$	= PROBABILITY of SYSTEM (S) SURVIVAL (= integrity, no undetected attacks) WHEN SUBJECTED to ATTACK "a" DURING INTERVAL "t"

$$Ig = 1 - (At\,(1 - S))$$

The SYSTEM INTEGRITY is RELATED DIRECTLY to the ATTACK FREQUENCY and the STRENGTH of SECURITY DESIGN for THOSE PARTICULAR ATTACKS

Example: ATTACK FREQUENCY 2% (.02), SECURITY DEGREE FOR THIS ATTACK 90% (.90)

$$Ig = 1 - (.02\,(1 - .90))$$

$$= .998 \quad \text{or} \quad 99.8\%$$

Note: THE TOTAL SYSTEM INTEGRITY IS GIVEN BY THE PRODUCT OF THE INTEGRITY VALUE FOR EACH ATTACK !

Fig 78. System integrity measures

SCALE VALUE	EXAMPLE
10	Uncontrolled large computer-based data banks with telecommunications, no security.
9	Telecommunication-linked computer systems with user-terminal password only.
8	Telecommunication-linked computer systems with terminal & file access control.
7	Telecommunication-linked computer systems with scrambled codes plus "8" above.
6	"Private wire (line)" systems using leased lines, e.g. banks.
5	Private wire systems using scrambled codes on the lines.
4	Computer-based systems operated by one company's staff only.
3	Computer-based systems, off-line & batch, relatively fast access, tandem operators.
2	Access to sensitive records controlled by lock & key. Key copies a problem.
1	Access to sensitive records controlled by combination lock or multiple keys - access by not more than 5 individuals.
0	Access to very sensitive file restricted to one person only, locked safes with one key only.

Fig 79. Taylor's Accessibility Scale.

Accuracy

Metric

a. "Freedom from error measure" (definition)

b. Notation: a = probable accuracy or measured accuracy
      Pr. (a) is better notation for probable accuracy.

c. Measurement: the ratio CORRECT DATA/ALL DATA = a.

d. Example: a system has 3 measured error-transactions for every 100
      transactions handled. The accuracy of the system =
      $a_S = 1 - (3/100) = 0.97$.

e. It should be noted that accuracy is a measure of "design adequacy"
   rather than "system reliability". Errors which influence this measure

are due to the data and the (assumedly correct) logic for processing that data. Additional (presumably rarer) error due to hardware failure (intermittent or hard) or logic "bugs" (intermittent or hard) is handled and measured separately under reliability concepts.

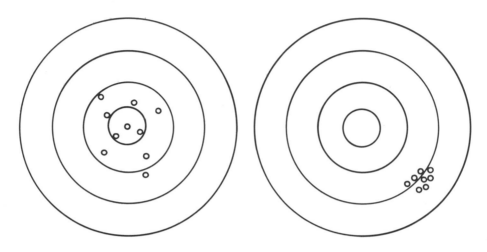

Target patterns of shots fired by two riflemen.

The left pattern shows low precision and high accuracy with large random errors.

The right pattern shows low accuracy and high precision with large bias (systematic error).

Fig 80. Accuracy and precision concepts. Adapted from Ivanov (1972) and A. Chapanis, 1951, "Theory and Methods for Analysing Errors in Man-Machine Systems" in Annals of N. Y. Academy of Sciences, vol. 51, p. 1179.

Accuracy - Concept Comments

Definition: A measure of the quality of freedom from error; the degree of exactness possessed by an approximation or measurement.

In contrast precision refers to the degree to which calculated results reflect theoretical values.

"Accuracy" was originally intended for numerical values but it seems useful to extend it to non-numerical information.

For example: My official name, as stated on my birth certificate and passport is "Thomas Steven Gilb". Anything like "Tom Gilb", "T. S. Gilb", etc. would be perfectly <u>accurate</u> but not fully <u>precise.</u>

By contrast: "Tomm Gill" or "T. D. Gilbo" are directly inaccurate (in addition to being less precise): "Thomas Stephen Gilb" has greater precision but is slightly inaccurate ("v" has become "ph"), a standard and transformable form of inaccuracy which will allow self-correction, by a program.

The following characteristics may be noted.

a. Data accuracy is a "reliability" concern. There are a multitude of possible "attacks" on data which result in some degree of error known as "inaccuracy". Data accuracy can therefore be improved by systematic design engineering, at a calculable cost.

b. Data accuracy measures can fruitfully be divided into degrees of inaccuracy according to the seriousness of the effect this inaccuracy is likely to have in a specific system. This gives a basis for value-oriented engineering design of <u>prevention, detection</u> and <u>correction</u> techniques related to the inaccuracy.

c. The degree of effort to be used in obtaining a certain degree of precision must always be evaluated in the light of the probabilities for the corresponding inaccuracy.

d. Rules for evaluating the seriousness of inaccuracy in some data may be determined by noting the degree of precision at the place of error.

Precision (in software)

a. Degree to which errors tend to have the same root cause.

b. <u>Notation</u>: Precision, logical precision

c. <u>Measurement</u>: $\text{Precision} = \dfrac{\text{number of actual errors (bugs) at source}}{\text{number of corresponding root errors (bugs)}}$
   observed in total which are caused by
   source bugs

d. <u>Example</u>: During time t_1 1 error (bug) causes 100 error messages. Precision = 0.01.

During time t_2 30 errors cause 60 error messages. Precision = 0.5. In 1 software-release period (t_3) 11,000 distinct errors cause 13,000 error reports. Precision (t_3) = 0.847.

e. Note: This proposed measure is an intuitive attempt to interpret the concept of precision in terms applicable to software and to practical measurement of the concept. It is an attempt to stimulate thinking in this area.

BUG CAUSE AND ITS EFFECTS

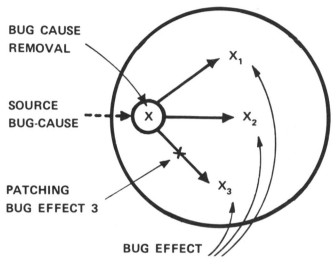

Fig 81. Software precision could be considered the ratio of source bugs to the effects they cause.

Error

a. Any deviation from a defined state of "correctness".

b. Measurement: in whole numbers of errors.

c. Example: About 11,567 software errors were reported for the 1972 version of IBM 370/Operating System.

d. Note: While error counts may be expressed fractionally ("1.5 bugs per line coded on the average") only whole number errors exist. Thus there is no such thing as half an error in judging whether a state is in error or not. An error is a binary concept (1 or 0).

Error detection probability

Pr. Detection$_e$ =

the probability (0.0000 to 1.0000) of detection of an error of type "e".

The detection environment must be specified:

for example, for data encoding methods,

- the general type of code used ("self-check mod. 11", etc.)
- the exact version used (number of characters, redundancy, etc.)
- the algorithm (program) used to detect inconsistency. Three general
  types of data error detection algorithm have been identified:
  - SELF-CONTAINED ALGORITHMIC
  - COMPARATIVE (FILE/TABLE REFERENCE)
  - COMMON SENSE (HUMAN LOGIC/MEMORY)
    (see GILB-READ-74 for more on this)

Error correction probability

Pr. Correction$_e$ =

same structure as Detection, above, except that the probability refers
to ability to reconstruct data in the form and content originally intended.

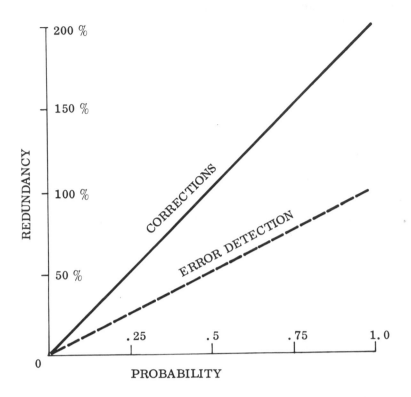

Fig 82. Hypothetical "experience" curves showing the relationship
between redundancy in for example a product number and the
detection/correction probability of errors.
The real values of such a relationship will be determined by
such parameters as the randomness of the valid product
numbers within the number (or alphabetic) series, the types
of algorithms used to detect and correct the errors.

Flexibility metrics

HOW MANY UNIQUE PATHS DOES THIS PROGRAM HAVE?

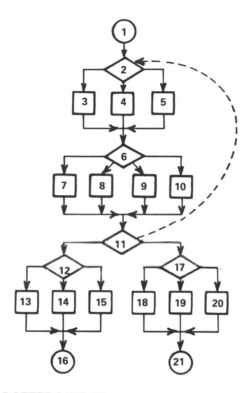

– WITHOUT THE DOTTED LINE 72

– WITH THE DOTTED LINE 93,748,416,840   or $72 + 72 \sum\limits_{n=1}^{12} \dfrac{12\,!}{(12-n)\,!}$

Assuming all paths independent

**Source: TRW–SS–73–01. Krause et al: Optimal Software Test Planning Through Automated Network Analysis.
TRW Software Series, One Space Park, Redondo Beach, CA 90278**

Fig 83. The number of theoretically possible logical path combinations in a program is another useful measure of logical complexity. It is objectively measurable by machine and gives insight into the number of potential test paths and untested parts of the program that could contain errors.

161

Logical complexity

a. Proposed indirect measure:

   - the number of "binary" decisions in the logic (absolute)

   - the ratio of absolute logical complexity to total logic (relative)

b. <u>Notation</u>: absolute logical complexity: C_L
                 relative logical complexity: c_L

c. <u>Measurement</u>: Automatic or manual measurement in the case of
   programming languages: the number of non-normal exits from a
   decision statement (IF, ON, AT END, etc.) gives the absolute
   logical complexity suggested measure. See Fig 58 i for such data.

   The relative logical complexity is the ratio of this to the total number
   of instructions.

d. <u>Experience note</u>: See FARR-75, where logical complexity (C_L) was
   found in a study to be a significant predictor factor for computer
   program cost. See "Practical Measurement of Logical Complexity
   of a Program" in Fig 46.

e. The value of this measure lies in its (intuitively assumed) potential
   as a convenient analytic tool for predicting and understanding relationships with other system properties (such as cost, effort, reliability,
   flexibility, maintainability, performance (speed/space)).

Logical complexity - Concept Comments

<u>Definition</u>: Logical complexity is a measure of the degree of decision-
making logic within a system.

<u>Example</u>: in a large computer program the absolute number of "IF"
(IF A = B THEN GO TO 22) statements gives a <u>rough</u> measure of the
logical complexity. If there were 1000 logical statements in the program
and 500 of these were "IF" then the logical complexity is probably far
higher than if there were only 10 "IF" statements.

If a written instruction for an office worker contains 30 options to fill
out/not fill out fields on a 100-field pre-printed form then the logical

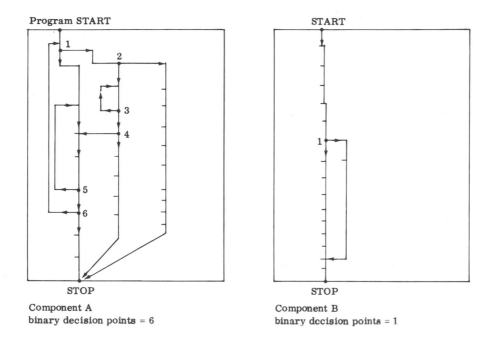

Fig 84. The concept of <u>logical complexity</u>. Is A more complex than B? Is this true if the total number of instructions in A is <u>239</u> and in B <u>10</u>?

complexity of that system (instruction form) is probably higher than a corresponding form where all fields are to be filled out.

Naturally, more complex measurements of the concept can be conceived of and justified for specific purposes.

a. The concept is interesting in data systems because experience tells us that there is some (largely unexplored) correlation between logical complexity and other important system characteristics such as error-proneness, cost, time.

b. The usefulness lies in giving us an <u>indirect</u> tool for analyzing, controlling and predicting these factors.

c. This supposition depends on the creation of appropriate measuring concepts that upon research show a high correlation with other system characteristics that are more difficult to measure, control and predict directly.

THE EFFECT OF COMPLEXITY SEEMS TO BE REDUCED PRODUCTIVITY
IN PROGRAM DEVELOPMENT

TYPE OF PROGRAMMED SYSTEM	PRO-GRAM UNITS	NUMBER OF PRO-GRAMMERS	ELAP-SED YEARS	TOTAL HUMAN-YEARS	PRO-GRAM WORDS PRODU-CED	WORDS/ HUMAN YEAR
OPERATIONAL CONTROL PROGRAM	50	83	4	101	52,000	515
MAINTENANCE CONTROL PROGRAM	36	60	4	81	51,000	630
COMPILER	13	9	2.25	17	38,000	2230
TRANSLATOR (DATA ASSEMBLER)	15	13	2.5	11	25,000	2270

BELL LABS DATA

POSSIBLE EXPLANATIONS: COMPLEXITY (number of modules,
                                                    control programs)
                         NUMBER OF PEOPLE INVOLVED

Fig 85. Source: F. J. Brooks: <u>The Mythical Man-Month</u>, Datamation.
         Dec. 1974 p. 49.

Built-in flexibility

Metric

a. Flexibility is useful complexity (in practice or potentially).

   To simplify, I call it "desirable complexity".

b. <u>Notation:</u> F   (F_S = Structural Flexibility), (F_L = Logical Flexibility)

c. <u>Measurement</u>: In general F = useful Complexity (an absolute measure
   relative F = useful C/total C (range 0 to 1. 0)

The <u>limit</u> of potential flexibility in any system is given by its complexity measures.

If all complexity is desired/useful then relative F = 1.

d. Naturally it is vital to <u>specify the reference point</u> (the set of system objectives, including constraints) against which the flexibility is being evaluated. It is only in this context that F has any significance.

e. One immediately obvious application of this measure would be in judging the suitability of "generalized" software packages against alternatives.

A low F ratio would indicate a potentially high "overhead" cost of using the system, a lack of suitability.

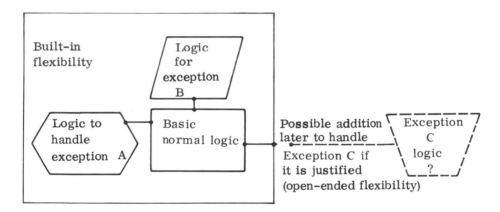

Fig 86. <u>Built-in flexibility</u>: system components which allow the system to handle variations immediately (within the system)

Built-in flexibility - Concept Comments

<u>Definition</u>: Built-in flexibility is the ability of a system to <u>immediately</u> handle <u>different</u> logical situations.

a. Built-in flexibility is foreseen in detail as a design requirement. The usefulness of being able to handle the situation immediately is judged as being high enough to justify an immediate investment in the logical component, or part, needed to handle the different situation.

This leads to the conclusion that all built-in flexibility must increase the system complexity proportionately. Further, it must be (or have been judged to be) "desirable", that is, intentional.

b. This leads to the conclusion that we can measure built-in flexibility if we can distinguish between "desirable/intended/useful" complexity and undersirable/unintended/useless complexity.

c. It is worth noting that since the concepts of "desirable and "useful" are both relative to some reference point and may even change in time, the measure of built-in flexibility may vary for a constant system while the measure of complexity will not.

d. As a simplification, in a recently designed system we can assume that all complexity is designed with some useful purpose in mind. We can therefore estimate initial measures of built-in flexibility to be almost equal to the complexity measure.

e. The ratio of flexibility to complexity would seem to give us a useful measure of the relevance of a system from a particular point of view or point in time. This would give us some basis for judging the desirability of redesigning and constructing a system component.

Example: a computerized system designed by the author produces output that will have worldwide distribution. It is designed with the built-in flexibility of producing output in Norwegian (the local language and destination of 50% of output) and English (for the rest of the world). It has been designed with open-ended flexibility for the addition of other languages by mere data additions and trivial logical changes.

A possible simplification might be to use a non-language such as numerics and abstract codes. Another simplification might be to preprint the languages on forms. Another might be to output both at once.

After several years' operation, it turns out that the flexibility of several more languages has not been utilized. Thus it falls into the category "undesired complexity" and the relevance of this flexibility is reduced.

Open-ended flexibility (adaptability)

Metric

a. It is not a simple matter to suggest a measure for this system property. The following suggestion must therefore be taken as tentative, perhaps as a starting point for understanding the nature of adaptability.

b. Latent adaptability is to some degree a function of the interfaces which are designed into it specifically to allow future change with relative ease. Logical interfaces are clearly connected with the idea of logical modules and their linkages. Each module linkage is an interface which may be useful for adapting the system.

   It becomes difficult indeed to see the distinction between structural complexity measures as suggested in this text, and a suitable indicator of adaptability.

c. I suggest that the number of "linkages" between modules is a relevant indicator of open-ended flexibility. It is a count of the number of places where changes can be "plugged in" without major disturbances in the existing system.

d. Notation: "I" (Interfaces)

e. Measurement: the same count of linkages between modules as for relative structural complexity ratio (linkages/modules) should serve as a practical gross indicator of the degree of interface.

   As pointed out, this can be automated for computer programs, thus a fast and consistent count is possible for large systems.

   Whether this in fact gives us a meaningful indicator, remains to be seen. See Fig 58 i (CALL Statements) for an example of automatic count.

167

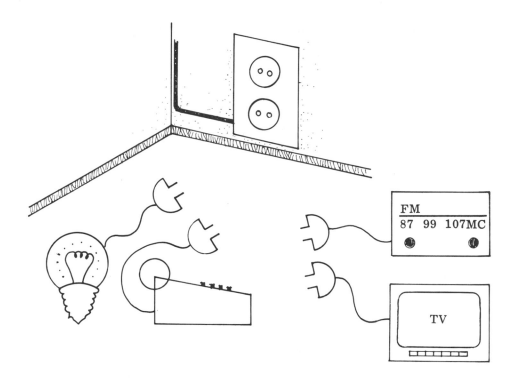

Fig 87. Open-ended flexibility is the concept of preparing for the future
by conscious design, with a minimum of present effort. It
usually involves preparing an <u>interface</u> with the future system
additions.

Flexibility (open-ended). Adaptability, Concept
Comment

<u>Definition</u>: Open-ended flexibility is a measure of the ease with which
new functions can be added to a system.

<u>Example</u>: It is envisaged that an academic periodical mailing list system
will have future potential as a selective book marketing data base. The
need or financial justification is not immediate, but is considered to be
highly probable.

A computerized mailing list system is designed and constructed with
such future use in mind and at a limited extra cost. The intended result
is that the marketing system can be added on, even though detailed design
specifications do not exist, without the need for a total or major redesign

of the basic periodical mailing list system. Many details of the basic system contribute to this flexibility, and all such decisions are taken on the basis that this will best satisfy the known objective of this probable general development (marketing system integration). For example: 1) Adequate space is allocated in the computer records for additional data for each subscriber and periodical. 2) Hardware is selected and dimensioned to cover the probable major increase in processing volume. 3) A decision to computerize the mailing procedure, as opposed to semi-automatic name-plate methods, is made in spite of the fact that name-plates give the best system efficiency when looked at in isolation from integration with probable future marketing applications.

One comparable concept is the way FM radios are often "prepared for" stereo FM, or the way cars are prepared for safety belts.

a. Open-ended flexibility is interesting since it may be an explicit design objective. The techniques needed to achieve it for specific categories of "unknowns" (about which some general knowledge is available) are not at present systematically recognized as a significant cost element either in immediate system design or in system redesign.

b. By recognition of the concept we expect to be able to learn to exercise greater control over present and future system costs.

c. The more general concept of system flexibility involves the concept of adaptability to a changing environment. Open-ended flexibility is a technique for approaching unclear future problems on a probabilistic basis.

Tolerance (of system input variation)

Metric

a. A system's input data tolerance is a measure of the system's ability to accept different forms of the same information as valid.

b. Notation: $\text{Tol}_s (v)$ or Tol_s,
   meaning the degree of tolerance for input data variation which system "s" has for variations of type "v".

c. Measurement: "v" may be variations such as:

- input medium (tape, card, display terminal)
- format (fixed, free form, graphic)
- logical variations of redundant representation such as abbreviations, misspellings, synonyms.

The quantity Tol_s is the number of permissible variations which will be accepted by the system s and handled in some sensible manner without being rejected as incomprehensible.

If the measure refers to a single unit of information then the quantity is a whole number from 0 to infinity. If it refers to a group of informational units then the average Tol_s for these may be given. For example, $Tol = 2.6$.

d. <u>Example</u> (hypothetical): A normal COBOL programming language compiler permits abbreviation and variation in the same concept in the order of $Tol_{COBOL} = 1.1$.

This is inconvenient for people who actually code and write programs. They need greater input tolerance so that the system will allow them to abbreviate certain concepts at will. To accept certain obvious misspellings as valid is a desired system tolerance for such a program compiler.

To remedy this situation, a number of "pre-compilers" have been developed which allow a large number of abbreviations and even certain misspellings.

$Tol_{COBOL\ precompilers}$ (abbreviations, frequent misspellings) = = 1.8 to 2.5.

Tolerance (input tolerance, input data tolerance).
Concept Comments

<u>Definition:</u> Tolerance describes the ability of a system to withstand a degree of variation in "input" without malfunction or rejection.

a. Tolerance design is a technique for increasing various measures of system effectiveness.

b. The principle methods of designing tolerant systems are:
- accepting a <u>number</u> of common <u>variations</u> as valid data to represent

CONCEPT OF TOLERANCE

Examples

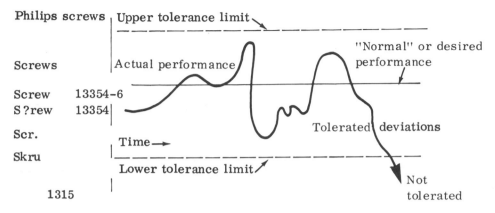

Fig 88. Tolerance can be planned into the design of a system so as to
provide greater result productivity and less delay whenever
deviations can reasonably be automated. For example: all
meaningful variations, misspellings and abbreviations of a
product identification may be automatically tolerated in order
to reduce order handling delays and coding costs. For example:
SCREW, 13354-6, 13354, SREW, SKRU, S?REW, SCR, could
all be tolerated as product identification (or classification) for
a particular product, as long as they cannot be confused with
other designations.

 the same information (instead of insisting on one unique code),
- including probability-oriented logic that enables a system to make
"safe" corrections to data that would otherwise be rejected or
handled wrongly.

c. Tolerance can be designed into any system to a greater or lesser
extent, giving a measurable cost and effect.

d. Tolerance becomes desirable when its cost is small compared to the
cost (or perhaps impossibility) of direct control of the source data
environment or when the time losses due to correction procedure are
intolerable or costly.

e. Tolerance may be oriented towards hardware variations or software
variations (for example accepting data from both cards and tape
encoders, or accepting several different COBOL source languages
by a single compiler). However one of the most interesting techniques
is humanization of systems by consistently asking the following

questions during design phases: "What is the most natural input language for the people who will in fact be communicating with the system? Which variations will it be possible and desirable to program the system to accept?".

This is very different from the early "people must adapt to computers" approach and reflects a change in the cost ratio of machines and people.

f. Input tolerance is a subcategory of the broader concept of built-in flexibility.

For practical design techniques see Gilb: <u>Data Engineering</u>, Studentlitteratur, and Gilb and Weinberg: Humanized Input (working title) Winthrop 1976.

g. John F. Myers' paper 012146-2-T, 1974, "Computation-Based Reliability Analysis" (Dept. of Electrical and Computer Engineering, Univ. of Mich.) suggests a tolerance relation concept: system fault tolerance degree.

Generality

Metric

a. <u>Notation</u>: G_s (e)   The applicability of system "s" to environment "e".

b. <u>Measurement</u>: G varies between 0.0 and 1.0 (100% applicability to the environment).

The actual measurement is subjective in most cases, but more objective <u>criteria</u> can be constructed, such as distinguishing <u>proved-and-tried</u> generality of s from <u>expected</u> generality of s.

Generality - Concept Comments

<u>Definition</u>: Generality is the degree to which a system is applicable in different environments.

a. To be meaningful it is necessary, therefore, to specify the universe of environments against which a systems generality is being evaluated.

For example a General Ledger Software Package may have great
generality, but it is crucial that we specify whether we mean
- for all countries
- for all industries
- for all General Ledger applications within our multi-industry
  corporation
- etc.

b. The concept of generality is thus the degree of applicability of a
system within a stated environment.

Portability

Metric

a. Notation: Portability = the ease of conversion of a system from one
environment to another; the relative conversion cost for a given
conversion method or algorithm. See Fig 89.

b. Portability is an "economic" concept, although the resources that
are measured, or that are of primary interest, are not necessarily
money. They may for example be manpower, time or machine
resources if these are the "bottlenecks" of primary interest.

c. Measure: $P_S = 1 - \dfrac{\text{resources to move "S" to target environment } (E_T)}{\text{resources needed to create "S" for resident environment } (E_R)^{*}}$

$$P_S = 1 - (E_T/E_R)$$

The conversion method or algorithm must be stated (experienced
human, program).

d. Example: A system "S" has cost 100, 000 money units to build for
operation within a certain environment (say IBM/370 135, DOS) and
the estimated maximum cost discounted in current money value for
moving it to a new environment (say Univac 1110, X8) is 10, 000
money units.

---

* Correctly; creation cost in target environment without benefit of
original "S".

173

$P_s = 1 - (10,000/100,000) = .9000$

Portability is 90%.

e. This concept is very useful for evaluating the full effect of a system design for systems which are expected to be moved in the near future, or where the worst case (conversion) must be evaluated. It points out that portability comes in degree - that it is measurable and that it can be used as a system design objective. See GILB-720906.

f. For many software systems of both general (for example: "COBOL") and specific nature (the Boolean IF in FORTRAN) it would be useful to have the portability (between defined environments, of course) indicated as a characteristic. It should then be possible to make design decisions for subsystems which result, totally, in a given degree of portability.

g. The implication of this measure is that "portability" is assumed to be a linear function for non-trivial software. This is intuitive until we get evidence to the contrary. In other words a program of 100,000 statements, we assume, will take 100 times the conversion effort of a similar 1,000-statement program.

h. See Fig 30 for an example of a contract guaranteeing portability.

Portability. Concept Comments

<u>Definition</u>: Portability is a reflection of the ease with which a system can be moved from one environment to another.

a. Portability is a characteristic of a <u>system</u>. By contrast "<u>compatibility</u>" (next metric) characterizes the relationship portability-wise between two environments, for a class of systems.

b. By definition, the concept of portability involves the following minimun information:
   - the resident environment (from which it is moved)
   - the target environment (to which it is moved)
   - the system which is moved
   - the measure of the concept of "ease" (money, effort, time, reliability).

c. Portability is a system characteristic which may be fruitfully applied to many subsystems or system components found in the software

systems area. It is <u>applicable to logical programs</u>, but also to <u>human procedures</u>, <u>humans themselves</u> and <u>hardware.</u> The important criterion for deciding whether a portability concept is applicable and of interest is: "Can we influence the degree of portability by making alternative design decisions in these subsystems?"
It is important to include such a broad area of consideration, since any one design area may be a necessary part of achieving total–system portability. It would be an unfortunate suboptimization to consider logicware portability alone.

d. It is desirable to be able to <u>measure and control</u> the portability characteristic of a system or any component of that system during the design and implementation phases, for the same reason that <u>reliability</u> must be controlled. Lack of control will inevitably result in insufficient quality or even in unnecessary costs.

e. Systems with high portability have the following applications: 1) ability to transfer to <u>future environments</u> with ease, 2) ability to be spread to <u>multiple environments</u> (marketing software, for example), 3) ability to function in <u>back-up environments,</u> thus affecting <u>reliability</u>. A new environment does not necessarily imply geographical or time separation: it may be of interest to design critical applications (payroll, for example) so that they will function in a "crippled" computer (graceful application system degradation).

Compatibility

Metric

a. Compatibility is intimately related to the measure of portability. Whereas <u>portability</u> is a <u>system</u> characteristic of <u>transformation</u> between two environments, <u>compatibility</u> is the <u>average portability</u> for a number (or class) of systems being moved between two environments.

In other words it is the <u>relationship between two environments.</u>

b. <u>Notation:</u> $\bar{P}_{(r:t)}$ (r = resident environment, t = target environment)

where $\bar{P} = \sum_{i=1}^{n} P_i / n$ (arithmetic mean).

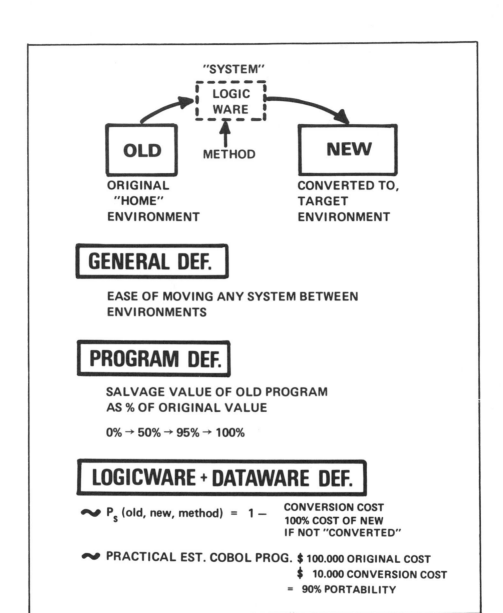

Fig 89. Portability metric.

176

Other statistical measures or ranges may be deemed more suitable for giving information about the average portability between the environments in question.

In any case, there is no need for concepts apart from the concept of portability to express the related concept of compatibility.

c. <u>Measurement</u>: Compatibility must be measured by a series of (average, maximum, minimum) portability measures, the purpose of which is to give information with which to predict future compatibility or to determine the degree of design-objective fulfilment.

d. <u>Example</u>: P is measured for systems moved between 2 environments A and B giving $P_{(i=1 \text{ to } 6)} = .4, .6, .5, .5, .9, .1$

$\bar{P}_{(A:B)} = .5$ (maximum .9 and minimum .1, 6 measured cases),

meaning that, on the evidence available, we can expect that the conversion of a system from environments A to B will cost 50% of the original development cost for A.

A and B are 50% compatible in general, with significant exceptions (which might be worth investigating before drawing any more conclusions).

Compatibility - Concept Comments

<u>Definition</u>: <u>Compatibility</u> is the measure of <u>portability</u> that can be expected of "systems" when they are moved from one given environment to another.

a. Compatibility will usually be in the form of a <u>generalization.</u> That is, it will usually refer to <u>classes</u> of environments (for example: IBM 360, IBM 370) and to a <u>class of systems</u> (all programs: COBOL program: ANSI Standard COBOL-74 etc).

Portability by contrast will normally refer to a single system or a more limited private collection of systems.

b. In practice only portability is directly measurable, although compatibility may be judged from the design specifications of the respective environments. Compatibility should be measured by means of statistical measures from several portability measurements.

c. Certainly it is useful to distinguish between theoretical compatibility (based on design) and measured compatibility based on a number of portability measurements of different systems that are moved between the same two environments. Design differences do not allow for the relative frequency with which incompatible features occur in real systems which are to be moved between different environments.

d. It is customary to distinguish between "levels" of compatibility, for example, hardware-level compatibility, assembly-language compatibility, high-level language compatibility, system external specification compatibility (forms, codes and operating procedures, i.e. human procedure compatibility).

e. Knowledge of the level of compatibility enables us to determine how portable a given system is or how portable it can be designed to be at a calculable cost. This is especially useful for designing portability to multiple environments into a system by finding the common compatibility factor among the environments and designing the system with that in mind.

f. Particular interfaces between subsystems may also be judged "compatible" or not compatible, for example calling-sequences for logical subroutines. These more or less compatible interfaces determine the portability of the subsystem, and are one possible criterion for judging the degree of portability of a system.

Structure metrics

<u>System: The thing we measure the structuredness of</u>

<u>Definition:</u> A complex set of related parts, methods or principles.

It is usually possible and useful to describe a system in terms of the objectives and constraints which are either pre-determined for it or to which it is apparently subject. This is not always possible in the real world, but for data systems it should always be possible.

From this we can deduce the definition: system = <u>purposeful, organized components.</u>

<u>Example:</u> Computer hardware, a project organization (in terms of people and methods), a computer program, codes and data (an "input language"), are all systems.

a. Any system is composed of subsystems. The lowest level of a system (which by choice or practical limitation is not analyzable into subunits) is a system part.

b. All subsystems (except "parts") are also systems at a more detailed level. They may exhibit different characteristics and be designed according to differently stated objectives than those of parent systems or daughter systems.

c. All systems in the real world may be assumed to have at least one parent system. That is, at least one "larger frame of reference" according to which their contribution can be judged in terms of relevant results rather than technical performance unrelated to specific objectives.

d. All systems can be described in terms of some <u>hierarchy</u> of systems, that is, not only their subsystems but also their supersystems or parent systems (the parent is the immediate supersystem).

This is basic to all system design, since <u>design is the process of selecting efficient systems and efficient hierarchical organizations of subsystems.</u>

e. A system has no direct measure, only a logical definition. The
   properties of systems are measurable and serve to describe the
   system, together with its functional (What does it do?) description.

THE SYSTEM

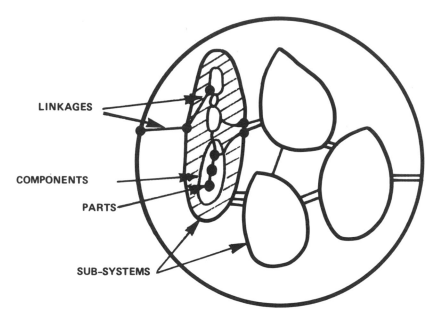

Fig 90. The concept of a system and its subdivisions into relatively
        more specialized compartments. Any single unit of this
        hierarchy is named according to its relationship to some other
        unit. At various points, then, any unit may be called any of
        the above terms (including "linkage").

Redundancy ratio

Redundancy (s, r) = quantity s/quantity r = Red.$_s$, where "s" is the
system being measured and r is some reference system.

If "r" is not specified, then it may be assumed to be the minimum
possible version of "s".

An adjective describing the type of redundancy intended must normally
be included in a definition of a particular case, for example, combinatorial
Red. , hardware Red. , character Red. , etc.

Red. $_s$ = 1.0 indicates that redundancy is at a minimum.

For example, if a code for a series of 1000 objects (customers, products) is six digits (000000 to 999999) then

Digit Redundancy $_s$ = 6/3 = 2.0

Combinatorial Redundancy $_s$ = 1,000,000/1000 = 1000.

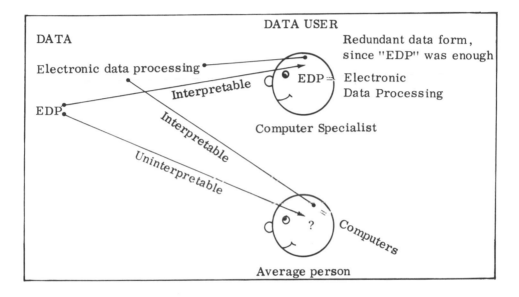

Fig 91. <u>Redundancy is a relative characteristic.</u> It must be determined by the data user characteristics and cannot be determined on the basis of the data (or system) alone.

Hierarchy

Metric

a. The basic measures of a hierarchy are
   - the depth or number of levels (H_L or H_{levels})
   - the total number of "nodes" or elements in the hierarchy (H_e or H_{nodes})
   - the number of elements at any one level of the hierarchy (breadth)

REDUNDANCY IS RELATIVE TO SPECIFIC CHARACTERISTICS WHICH
A DATA USER IS INTERESTED IN:

Interested in:

123-123

(compare the error version 123-128)

Pin-Pin-Pin

(compare the correctable error
version PIN-PAN-PIN)

CODE REPETITION REDUNDANCY
is not redundant from the error
detection point of view of the user,
but only from the information
point of view.

Code triplication is fairly
redundant from the detection
point of view but it enables us
to make an automatic self-
correction on a probability basis.
It is not redundant at all from
that point of view.

Fig 92. Redundancy and functional point of view.

b. In addition it is useful to have a notation to indicate the exact
location in a hierarchy from which a subhierarchy is being measured.

c. <u>Example:</u>

        0

     0 0 0

  0 00 0 0

H_L = 3 (including top and bottom levels)

H_e = 9

Note also that H_e/H_L = 9/3 = 3 gives a measure of the average breadth
of the levels (median breadth approx).

d. It is worth noting that this measure is related to the measure of
<u>structural complexity</u>, and certainly some of those measures are
also applicable to hierarchies.

NB. This is a proposal based on intuition. I expect to revise it as new
ideas come to my attention.

At the very least we have a quantitative hierarchy descriptor. Whether
or not it is productive is to be demonstrated.

REDUNDANCY $\longrightarrow$ ERROR DETECTION
$\longrightarrow$ ERROR CORRECTION

RELATIONSHIP

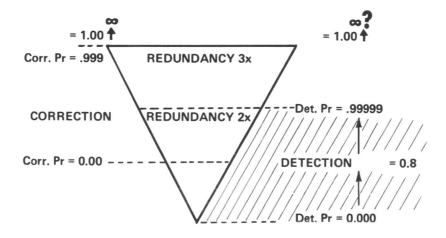

NOTE:

- THE REDUNDANCY REQUIREMENT FOR CORRECTION > THAT FOR DETECTION

- OUR ABILITY TO DESIGN SELF CORRECTING ATTRIBUTES INTO A SYSTEM IS DEPENDENT ON A HIGH DEGREE OF <u>DATA</u> REDUNDANCY (✚ suitable algorithms)

Fig 93. The diagram is based on observation and is only intended to indicate a tendency and not an exact rule.

Hierarchy. Concept Comments

Hierarchy (of data). Data may be arranged in groups which are related to each other. Any number of interesting levels may be included. There will always be one highest level containing a single group which represents the totality of data under consideration.

183

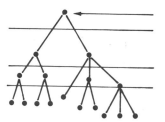

Level 1 (top, first etc.)

Secondary level of the hierarchy

Lowest level, most detailed level

Fig 94. <u>Hierarchy</u>: a simple "tree" (up-side-down) structure.

<u>Example</u>: a typical hierarchical conceptual data description is: data bank, comprising data bases, files, record types, individual records, fields, characters, bits, in that order.

The terms "tree-like" or "pyramidal" are often used to express this concept.

a. Hierarchical organization is important, since it allows us to handle parts of <u>complex structures</u> in terms of well-defined and related simplified groups. We can thus make <u>fewer detailed decisions</u> when creating a system and <u>save system design energy</u>.

b. This may result in some <u>loss of efficiency</u> when hierarchical categorization is inappropriately organized so that it puts components of <u>critically different natures</u> in the <u>same category</u> instead of assigning them to a separate group.

c. Hierarchical organization is both a tool for <u>analyzing</u> existing or proposed systems and for <u>describing</u> and organizing new systems (of data in this case).

d. The concept of hierarchy is a <u>tool</u> for handling complexity and may be a burden in cases which are already simple, where it should, of course, be avoided.

e. The reader is referred to Professor Langefors' principles (LANGE-FORS-THAIS) numbers 8, 10 and 11, pp. 49-62, for one explanation of the necessity of hierarchical design. Donald Knuth's works have other insights.

f. The major limitation of a hierarchy is that it has a "heart" at the top, that is, a critical point which if unreliable will destroy the entire system. In systems which must have a high availability, such as telephone systems, other ways of routing data must be designed into the system.

Structural complexity and structural simplicity

Metric

a. Suggested indices and notation:

C_S = absolute structural complexity = number of modules or subsystems

c_S = relative structural complexity = $\dfrac{\text{no. of module linkages}}{\text{no. of modules}}$ = L/m

b. Measurement: In some systems the measurement may be automatic (using a suitable analysis program) such as in FORTRAN programs, where the number of modules is conveniently the number SUBROUTINES + FUNCTIONS, and the number of linkages is the number of subroutine parameters + references to COMMON (as reflected in the COMMON statement in each subroutine).

Naturally there may be other structural concepts needing some measure (such as the subsystem or program level), which the reader can invent and verify the usefulness of. See Fig 51 for an example.

c. Example: In Fig 95,

System A (5 subsystems, 12 linkages) $C_S = 5$, $c_S = 12/5 = 2.4$

System B (2 subsystems, 7 linkages) $C_S = 2$, $c_S = 7/2 = 3.5$

Conclusion: Relative structural complexity is greater in system B, the absolute system complexity is greater in system A.

d. Cautionary note: Whether these measures mean as much as we intuitively suspect they do, is a matter for empirical research which still remains to be carried out at the time of writing. In other words, we have a basic idea which seems worth doing research on, but we do not know whether the concepts or the proposed measures are as useful as we hope they are. See the reference HOSKYNS-73 for related research data from practical modularization.

e. We should expect these concepts to be useful in indicating system maintainability and flexibility/adaptability as well as some other system properties.

185

f. Simplicity of structure can be measured by $1/C_S$ or $1/c_S$.

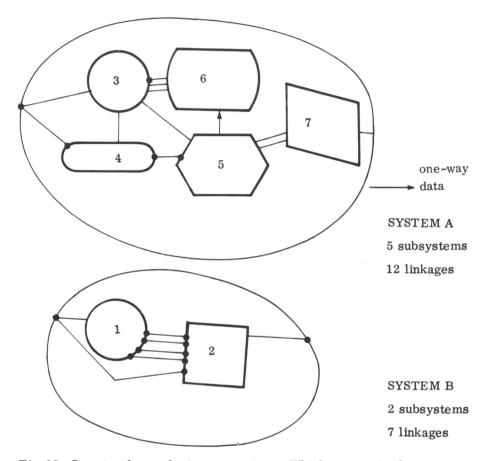

one-way
→ data

SYSTEM A

5 subsystems

12 linkages

SYSTEM B

2 subsystems

7 linkages

Fig 95. Structural complexity comparison. Which system is the "most complex" structurally? What basis is there for suspecting that structural complexity is related to system costs?

Structural complexity. Concept Comment

Definition: A measure of the degree of simplicity of relationships between subsystems.

Example: A system composed of three subsystems A, B, and C, where A controls B and C, obviously has a lower structural complexity than a ten-subsystem (A, B, C...I, J) system where any subsystem can communicate with any of the others.

HOW DO WE DIVIDE MODULES?
MODULARITY DIVISION CRITERIA

1. FREQUENCY OF OPERATIONAL USE
      CF COBOL SEGMENTATION

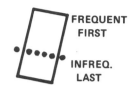

FREQUENT
FIRST

INFREQ.
LAST

2. PROBABILITY OF CHANGE IN MODULE

3. REFERENCE TO DATA IN SAME COLLECTION
      FILE, DB, RECORD, ELEMENT

4. MODULE SIZE
      "NOT MORE THAN A PAGE" or " $>$ 100 stmts"
      NOT MORE THAN 2K

5. MACHINE DEPENDENT FUNCTIONS (portability) DEVICE
      DEPENDENT

6. BY CALENDER SCHEDULE OF NEED OF MODULE

WHY DO WE DIVIDE ON ONE CRITERIA **?**

• • •

1. OPERATIONAL SPEED OPTIMIZATION

2. MAINTENANCE EASE

3. FILE PROCESSING OPTIMIZATION

4. HUMAN COMPREHENSION; DIVISION OF LABOR, MACHINE LIMIT (VS)

5. DIFFERENT SPECIALITIES & PROGRAMMERS

6. EARLY IMPLEMENTATION; EVOLUTIONARY PROJECT DEVELOP.

Fig 96. There are many different rules for dividing systems into
      modules. Each rule has one or more motives (Rule 1 above
      has a corresponding "WHY" 1 below). Each rule can conflict
      with the other modularization rules and with other design
      criteria. Resolution of the conflict can be achieved by a
      clearly stated set of priorities, for example, as in a MECCA
      model, using percentages.

At the same time this information tells us <u>nothing</u> whatsoever about the <u>logical complexity</u> of any of these systems or subsystems.

a. The concept is of interest for the same reasons that logical complexity is. We suspect, from practical experience of systems, that this factor is correlated with other, less controllable, less predictable, less planable, functions (cost, reliability, etc.). See FARR Fig. 46.

b. We further suspect (for both types of complexity: logical and structural) that these concepts can profitably be described in both absolute and relative terms, since relative complexity measures give us a better comparison basis with different sizes of systems, while absolute complexity measures may relate to some important real world constraints such as human conceptual or human organizational ability.

c. I have been unable to find experiments that demonstrate the usefulness of these concepts. The most relevant work is that of Myers in "Composite Design: The Design of Modular Programs" (IBM TR 0024 06, 1973) and in his book <u>Reliable Software through Composite Design</u> (Petrocelli, 1975, ISBN 0-88405-284-2). Unfortunately Myers's work is not based on any quantitative data, but solely on intuitive reasoning. He does, however, recognize degrees of module structure and the multidimensional effects that these degrees of module coupling probably have. He also states clearly that he does not know the influence of different degrees of module-coupling on most of the possible resulting attributes of the modules.

Modularity

Modularity implies

- division of a system "s" into a number of "modules" (the more of these, the more modularity). Modules can be interpreted as subsystems <u>immediately</u> below the level of the system "s" (i.e. its main components).
- that these modules have a limited interface to any other subsystems (in or outside of "s"). The less the interface the greater the degree of modularity. The interfaces are characterized by one or more <u>linkages</u> (as discussed under Structural Complexity linkages).

Modularity is just another term for structural complexity.

A thorough quantitative handling of the characteristics and attributes of modular programs is found in HOSKYNS - 73.

MULTIDIMENSIONAL EFFECTS OF MODULAR PROGRAM DESIGN

ASK: IN WHAT DIRECTION DOES PROPOSED MODULARIZATION AFFECT PROGRAM ATTRIBUTES?

DO WE <u>KNOW</u> THE DEGREE OF EFFECT?
OR ARE WE GUESSING?

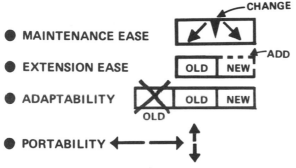

- ● MAINTENANCE EASE

- ● EXTENSION EASE

- ● ADAPTABILITY

- ● PORTABILITY

- ● OPERATIONAL EFFECTIVENESS

- ● GENERALITY OF USE IN DIFFERENT APPLICATIONS

- ● CONSTRUCTION COST

- ● PREDICTABILITY OF TOTAL PROGRAM COSTS & QUALITY USING "KNOWN" MODULES

- ● TESTING EASE (LIMITING EFFECT OF CHANGE)

Fig 97. Modularity is a structural property of software (including data-ware!), which seems to be related to a number of interesting metrics. Myers (in MYERS-CD-73) explicitly stated that he did not know the effect of his proposed modularity rules on most of these attributes.

189

= AS SEEN AND UNDERSTOOD BY PROGRAMMER

```
COBOL                                    FORTRAN ,PL/I etc.

                                         PROC MAIN;

A' SECTION.
    PARAGRAPH—1.                         CALL A
        IF ~~~~~~~~~~
        AND ~~~~~~~~~
        SUBTRACT ~~~~~~ .                CALL A-ENTRY (1, B3, F)


  ~ ~ ~ ~ ...... END OF MODULE

    PARAGRAPH—2.                         CALL B (A, C, B1)
                                         END PROC MAIN;
                                         — — — — — — — — — — New page

    PARAGRAPH—3.                         SUBROUTINE A

BB SECTION.                              END A;
                                         — — — — — — — — — New page



                                         SUBROUTINE B (C, D, X)

    PERFORM PARAGRAPH—1.                 A-ENTRY.

                                         END B;
    PERFORM PARAGRAPH—1 THRU
        PARAGRAPH—3.

    GO TO PARAGRAPH—2
```

Fig 98. Program module clarity as it affects the tendency to allow human error during program coding to go undetected by compilers, is a clear enough concept when we examine these examples. No quantified research is known, however.

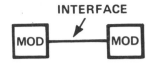

INTERFACE

MOD — **MOD**

DEGREES OF MODULARITY

● **NUMBER OF INTERFACES TO OUTSIDE**

● **TYPE OF INTERFACE**

● **CLARITY OF MODULE BOUNDARY**

● **STRENGTH OF MODULE BOUNDARY**

Fig 99. Intuitively, there seem to be 4 major concepts which are somehow measurable, which reflect the degree of the concept of modularity (see also MYERS-CD-73 and his book Reliable Software Through Composite Design, Petrocelli).

Distinctness

Software "distinctness" is a measure of the failure-point independence of a piece of software which is performing the same function as another piece of software. It is analogous to hardware distinctness, which is utilized in dual hardware systems, which perform the same task, and rarely fail at the same instant.

The measuring tool is the rate of failures which occur in a single software module compared to the total rate of failures.

$$\text{Distinctness Degree} = \frac{\text{number of bugs in module-1 alone}}{\substack{\text{number of bugs in module-1 which} \\ \text{simultaneously occur in module-2}}}$$

As far as I know, the term was first used in a paper by Lockheed Research (reference FISCHLER-74 and earlier papers by this group).

The classes of errors which are detectable and correctable using distinct software are shown in Fig 100 and the principal techniques for modifying the degree of distinctness are shown in Fig 101.

For related concepts see the section on Dual Code in Part I (Fig 44).

RELATION OF DISTINCT SOFTWARE TO DESIGN ERRORS

Design errors leading to system errors	Correction or detection via distinct software
● Improper translation of problem specifications	Two programming teams each starting with the given system specifications
– Wrong computation or wrong action taken due to misinterpreting the specifications in software or hardware	
● Resource problems	Rearranging processing order of in-dependent procedures
– Real-time combination of requirements and allocation of available resources causes deadlock or delay in processing. Reconfiguration of redundant system after partial failure, not properly designed	
● Numeric	Use equivalent standard mathematical routines. Rearrangement of computation flow, e.g. $a+b-c$ to $a-c+b$
– Computational routine fails for a set of values of variables Software logic fails for some variable values	
● Order code error	Any method of distinctness that assures different data-set/computer-state combinations (as a function of time) during task execution
– For certain combinations of computer state and data items, wrong action is taken by the computer (e.g., improper register load, erroneous transfer, etc.)	
● Timing	
– Delay of input signal processing causes hangup of system, with subsequent obsolete and perhaps contradictory data used.	
– Improper interaction of two signals causes erroneous action to take place	
– Erroneous estimate of processing time causes missed deadlines	
● Transmission of data	Use conventional error detection/correction codes, or comparison of duplicated data. Attach source and destination labels to transmitted data
– Wrong origin or destination used	
– Improper read or write to memory. Handshaking signals ambiguous in certain timing situations	
● Software	Compare results of distinct program to detect errors. Invoke standby distinct software for error recovery
– Design errors leads to software/data damage during program execution	
– Error detection and isolation techniques inadequate	

Fig 100. Distinctness Categories. Source: M.A. Fischler, O. Firschein and D.L. Drew, Distinct Software: an Approach to Reliable Computing.

192

PRINCIPAL TYPES OF SOFTWARE DISTINCTNESS

Technique	Advantages	Disadvantages
• Alternative global algorithms	• Complete data set-computer state distinctness	• Comparison points may be difficult to find • Programming expense [a]
• Alternative standard mathematical routines	• Routines may be already coded, saving programming expense	• Exact comparison may be difficult due to different round-off properties (equivalence ranges must be provided)
• Separate teams of programmers using same functional specifications	• Complete data set-computer state distinctness	• Programming expense [a]
Rearrangement of processing order		
• High level Process A, B Process B, A	• Better data set-computer state distinctness than low level • Can be done automatically	• May be difficult to determine parallelism
• Low level $c - a + b \rightarrow b + c - a$	• Can be done automatically	• May have a minimal effect on distinctness
• Alternative compilers	• Automatic • Low cost if compilers are already available	• Possible communication problems between routines produced by different compilers

(a) May be balanced out by decreased testing costs.

Fig 101. Distinctness Categories. Source: M.A. Fischler, O. Firschein and D. L. Drew, Distinct Software: An Approach to Reliable Computing.

Performance metrics

Effectiveness

a. Effectiveness is a group measure comprising:
   - operational reliability
   - system readiness
   - design adequacy.

b. It is expressed as the "probability that the system can successfully meet an operational demand within a given time when operated under specified conditions" (Welker in IRESEN, 1-7). See Fig 68.

c. Notation: "E". E = system Effectiveness.

d. Example: If system readiness probability = 0.90 (A, simplified) and system reliability probability = 0.99 (R) and design adequacy (example: accuracy) = 0.99 (a), then system effectiveness is limited by and is the product of these probabilities = 0.8821 = E.

Efficiency

Definition: Efficiency is the ratio of useful work performed to the total energy expended. It could also be expressed as the effectiveness/cost ratio.

a. The importance of the concept is that it provides us with a design/ engineering tool. We can select alternative design components on the basis that they satisfy the following requirements: 1) minimum of effectiveness, 2) not exceeding the maximum cost, and 3) greatest efficiency of the alternatives that have satisfied 1) and 2).

b. It is obviously important that we have a clear notion of the theoretical and practical difference between the concept of efficiency (which includes the idea of variable running cost or energy) and effectiveness (which includes "output" only). The importance of these concepts in any given design situation is determined relative to the appropriate goals and limitations specified for the design, since these are usually formulated in effectiveness and cost terms.

For example: The _effectiveness_ of triple verification of data registration by independent operators is probably high, but its _efficiency_ is so low as to make it undesirable except in cases where it is the only available method of achieving the required minimum _effectiveness_ (in terms of _accuracy_ in this case).

Another example: high redundancy data registration language designs, such as humanized texts instead of abstract numeric codes, are probably effective in terms of error detection and correction (i. e. accuracy) but the efficiency (of the computerized subsystem, at least) may be lower if the data must be interpreted by a series of machines and humans, since the _transformation_ (computer interpretation) of humanized data into useful information (encoding "JONES" to a unique number, for example) may cost an order of magnitude more than simple computer transformations at the _beginning_ of the process.

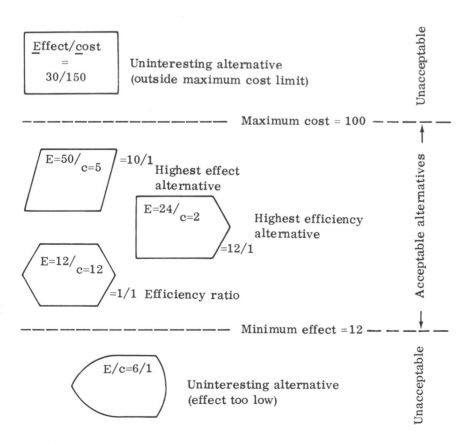

Fig 102. _Efficiency_ as a tool for selection of alternatives.

195

Transformation work

a. A transformation measure is the <u>energy</u> or <u>resources</u> needed to convert data from some original state to its "transformed" state.

b. The measurement may be made directly in terms of resources (money, time, manpower, electricity, etc.) or energy (logical cycles).

c. Any measurement, to be meaningful, should specify:
   - the original state of the data
   - the final state of the data
   - the units of energy or resources measured
   - the accuracy of the measurement
   - the algorithm used to perform the transformation.

d. <u>Notation</u>: "T"

   T_{cycles}, $T_\$$, $T_{nanosec}$, etc. "T" alone may be useful for expressing relative T, for example: T (decimal to binary) = T (binary to decimal) for system x.

e. <u>Measurability</u>: This should normally be extremely good in terms of work cycles or time, since machines can be used for direct measurement and calculation.

f. It seems obvious that this measure is of importance for calculating or measuring the effect, in terms of "performance", of changes made to algorithms, procedures, machine modules, etc.

   It would seem useful to have a large number of tables on standard transformations available to the data systems engineer.

g. <u>Note</u>: This measure is reflected at the "system" level by the concept of "<u>portability</u>" (P).

ESTIMATED TYPICAL TRANSFORMATION ENERGY (relative logical cycles)

BETWEEN COMMON QUANTIFIER DATA FORMATS

FROM	1	.1	1/1	ND	AL	PO	GR	DE	IN
WHOLE NO. 1	1	7	2	2	2	3	30	2	2
DECIMAL .1	5	1	7	7	7	8	35	7	7
FRACTION 1/1	12	10	1	14	14	15	42	14	14
NON-DEC. ND	11	18	13	1	13	14	41	13	13
ALPHA AL	30	37	32	32	1	33	60	32	32
POSITION PO	20	27	22	22	22	1	50	22	22
GRAPHICAL GR	200	207	202	202	202	203	1	202	202
DEFAULT DE	3	10	5	5	5	6	33	1	5
INTERNAL IN	2	9	4	4	4	5	32	4	1

Fig 103. A very crude estimate of the typical amount of logical (computer program) energy needed to transform one quantifier data format to another.

Cautionary note: This table is shown solely to illustrate how the transformation concept could be used to give design information in table form. Developed in 30 minutes from a subjective estimate of the number and type of computer program steps and time needed to make the conversion. A number of assumptions had to be made which will not be stated here (example: microprogramed two-way conversion from internal formats). This should, however, give the reader a better overview of the wide variations in transformation energy between quantifier data formats.

Hopefully, this table will be considerably improved by more careful study of the necessary algorithms. In any case considerable variations may be expected depending on the algorithm-performing device (human, computer-type).

See Fig 49 for other attributes of these data element design options. A detailed discussion of these design alternatives will appear in forthcoming books by this author.

Transformation (of data)

Definition: The process of changing data from one form to another form.

The following interesting categories of transformation occur:

- logically reversible transformations
- transformations which result in equivalent information when both data forms are interpreted by a specific algorithm (or group of people, for example)
- the opposite cases of the above two categories
- border cases, such as when data is transformed to other data forms which describe a broader category of information.

a. Transformation is a process carried out by some (formal or informal) algorithm.

b. There is usually (always?) more than one possible transformation algorithm for two sets of data forms (from/to forms).

c. Each of these different transformation algorithms will have different characteristics (size, speed, reliability, portability, cost, etc.)

d. A transformation will require a variable quantity of "energy", depending upon the characteristics of the two data forms involved and the efficiency of the algorithm, as well as the capabilities of the algorithm machine (which may be a human).

e. It is possible to predict to some degree of accuracy the energy (in terms of cost, time, other resources of critical interest) needed for a transformation, when we know the data forms. This gives us the general requirements for this transformation on the basis of some "best" algorithm. If we know which machine or human will perform the transformation then we can be more accurate or specific in our calculation of transformation energy.

f. Thus, design of systems must consider the data formats as one variable design factor for influencing final system characteristics. The system designer must be able to understand the energy consequences of variations in data forms which occur outside and inside his system, since data processing is characterized by constant transformation of data forms.

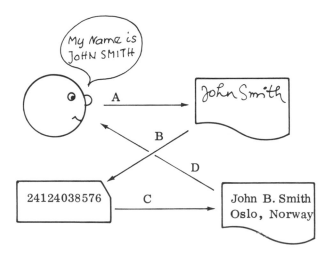

Fig 104. Transformation: Four logically reversible transformations (A, B, C, D). Can you think of at least two different ways in which <u>each</u> transformation can be carried out? Can you estimate the time, cost and reliability of each suggested way?

Resource metrics

Financial datametrics

Purpose: Most financial parameters should be thoroughly specified at
the point at which they are used so that they are unambiguous and can
be compared with any other interesting concepts.

This specification of financial datametrics is to give computer scientists
some bare minimum common reference terminology, and students some
basis for differentiation into the most interesting categories.

Total system cost

$\$_s(t)$, $£_s(t)$, currency symbol$_{system}$(time)

In _any_ cost estimate, we must state the currency referred to (even if it
is in "relative financial units" which are relative to each other only),
the exact system definition (which should have very clear borders), and
the time period for which the amount is relevant (t).

Total system cost should be defined so that the reader of the figures
need be in no doubt as to which costs are included and which costs are
not.

It is good practice to make this quite clear by specifically stating the
criteria for and examples of costs inside and outside of the limits laid
down.

It is also good general practice to indicate the _reliability_ of the estimates.

For example:

Total system cost for a payroll program:

Expressed in U. S. Dollars (of 740101), the system in the program numbered
2456-PY, the time period is 740110 to 760326. The costs are all direct
EDP department costs as shown by the department accounting and time
sheets, for people and machines involved in the project for analysis,
design, programming and maintenance. Fixed overheads are included
on a proportional basis - in proportion to the variable costs. Not included are time and facilities of outside departments such as financial

management, payroll clerks, and employee time. The costs are accurate to about 5% variation due to estimates and inaccuracies in recording.

Clearly inadequate would be the formulation:

The payroll EDP costs were twice as high as the previous system.

HOW MUCH WILL THE PROGRAM COST **?**

SOFTWARE COST/TIME/ RESOURCE PLANNING <u>MINIMUM</u> REQUIREMENTS

● KNOW INDIVIDUAL PRODUCTIVITY

26 : 1
WORST   BEST
TIME

● KNOW PRODUCT DESIGN DEMANDS: EXACTLY

FINISH DATE — PORTABILITY

PROBABILITY OF MAINTAINABILITY$_s$ = **95%** in 10 min.

RELIABILITY

● KNOW PRODUCTION METHOD   "STRUCTURED DUAL CODE"
ENVIRONMENT   TEAM PROGRAMMING
MOTIVATION   STRONG POSITIVE REWARD **$**

● EXPERIENCE DATA WITH ABOVE FACTORS: TIME (RANGE): SOFTWARE ENGINEERING HANDBOOK TABLES

ABOUT

● BREAK DOWN LARGE ESTIMATION OBJECTS INTO SMALLER ONES

IT STILL WON'T BE EASY; BUT, YOU WILL UNDERSTAND HOW BAD YOUR ESTIMATE IS **!**

Fig 105.

Incremental costs

$$d\$_s(t)$$

d = incremental cost
$\$$ = the relevant currency symbol (N. kr., Hfl, YEN, A$\$$)
s = the system in question
t = the time period for which the change is applicable, which may be
     expressed in international standard dates and time (for example
     771224.2100 means Dec 24 1977 at 9 pm, local or GMT)

An incremental cost is the additional cost as a result of some change
such as:

- an additional time period which has elapsed

- a change in the system (program change, person change)

- a change in the environment outside the system as defined by "s".

Capital investment - capital $\$_s(t)$

Capital investment is a particular type of "total system cost". In general
it is the costs incurred before operation of the system, which are in-
curred whether or not the system actually succeeds in becoming operational.
In general these costs will be spread for purposes of accounting. taxation
and real cost evaluation, throughout the assumed, actual or legal (taxation
law) life of the system.

Capital costs can generally be converted into running variable operational
costs at the will of the designer of the system - at least this is one design
option that usually deserves consideration. The conversion is
accomplished by either transferring the responsibility to outside parties,
or by accepting an operational cost penalty which could have been avoided
by additional initial capital outlay (such as better program design, which
could reduce operational machine capacity costs).

Usually, it is uninteresting to see capital (or "initial outlay") costs in
isolation from the running operational costs of the system. This can
easily result in misleading impressions. Both costs should be shown at
the same time to anyone who is expected to evaluate them.

DATA BASE ATTRIBUTES

- **MAINTAINABILITY:** HOW FAST CAN WE FIX IT WHEN ERROR STRIKES?

- **ADAPTABILITY:** HOW EASILY CAN IT CHANGE TO MEET NEW CONDITIONS?

- **PORTABILITY:** HOW MUCH CONVERSION EFFORT NEEDED TO MAKE IT WORK IN NEW HARDWARE OR SOFTWARE ENVIRONMENT?

- **RELIABILITY:** TO WHAT DEGREE CAN WE RELY ON THE CORRECTNESS AND AVAILABILITY OF THE DATA WHICH IT IS DESIGNED TO HOLD?

- **OPERATIONAL COST:** MACHINE COST, SOFTWARE (maintenance!) COST

- **IMPLEMENTATION COST:** HOW MUCH TIME AND PEOPLE TO GET IT GOING?

- **LIFE SPAN:** WHAT IS IT'S EXPECTED USEFUL LIFE ("half-life")

- **APPLICATION PROGRAMMER COST:** HOW DOES IT AFFECT THESE LARGE STAFF COSTS?

- **SUPPORT:** HOW MANY YEARS WILL THE SOFTWARE BE SUPPORTED? Etc.

- **DATA RETRIEVAL SPEED:** SINGLE ITEM AT RANDOM, REPORT, DB SCAN. HUMAN CONVENIENCE VS MACHINE EASE

- **COST GROWTH CONTROL:** WILL CHANGES MADE BY EXTERNAL SUPPLIER FORCE YOU INTO EXTRA HARDWARE AND MAINTENANCE COSTS?

- **AUTOMATION DEGREE:** TO WHAT DEGREE ARE RELATED WORK PROCESSES AUTOMATED OR DEPENDENT ON HUMAN LABOR? FOR EXAMPLE: APPLICATION DESIGN, REORGANIZATION, ERROR DETECTION, ERROR CORRECTION, ERROR DIAGNOSIS AND AUDITING, METERING/INSTRUMEN-TATION.

- **SECURITY:** TO WHAT DEGREE IS DATA SECURE FROM MISUSE AND ALTERATION?

Fig 106. Resource metrics are some of the most critical attribute descriptors for data base management logicware and dataware. (See GILB:DBS-73)

Operational cost – operational $\$_s(t)$

This is the cost incurred by the existence of the system (s) through any time period (t) specified.

This cost will usually vary depending on system activity. It may specifically include "amortized capital costs", so that a more realistic picture of the operational costs is presented.

In this case the rate ("written off evenly over 5 years") at which the capital investment is written off should be clearly indicated.

Return On Investment (ROI) - $ROI_s(t)$

This is the plus or minus return on investment for the system "s" during or up to time period "t". The ROI expresses the ratio of system value/system cost (including investment capital and operational cost).

The exact formulation of this is a matter for local accounting practices in your institution or company. See Steiner, Top Management Planning, page 372, Collier-MacMillan, Canada, 1969 or most financial management textbooks for discussions of ROI use and abuse.

The value of the system to its users may be based on a combination of objective and subjective criteria. System value is a measure of the "value of its existence" and can be used as a tool to exercise control over the cost/value ratio of operational systems (practiced by BHP, Melbourne, for example, in all corporate EDP). See GILB:CTC-1974 "Dynamic Return on Investment".

Time resource datametrics

Time resource datametrics may seem to be so obvious as not to need special definition or clarification. In fact the same terms used by different people can have quite different meanings. In the interests of accuracy we must define our terms clearly - so that experiments can be repeated, for example.

Computer Time

The computer time used to run a particular program (or set or subset of one) must be specified so that it cannot be misinterpreted, and so that others will obtain the same result if the same run is repeated under the same conditions.

If the time is measured as total elapsed effective time of a part of the computer machinery, then this must be specifically stated, for example "30.3 seconds elapsed CPU time as measured by the computer clock and printed out at the end of the experiment".

Certainly the specification of which overhead costs are included or not included in the timing is of importance for the evaluation of the time given. It must be clear whether the timing is affected by the cost of reloading and initializing programs that are frequently interrupted. It must be clear whether the operating system overheads are included in any way, and if they aren't they should almost certainly be specified separately in some manner (program load, general overheads, linkage loader timing).

The estimated accuracy and repeatability of the measure should be indicated.

In most cases where net machine resource usage timings are given, it would be fair to the reader of such numbers to also indicate the wall clock/calender elapsed time, and the reasons for any differences in the two timings.

Human time

The Man-Year. Software engineering results frequently involve the concept of man-years (supposed to mean one person's working year), or similar concepts such as man-hours, man-months, man-weeks. These concepts measure expended energy for ordinary elapsed time in conventional calender/clock measures. For example: he used 300 man-hours during a 6-month period. The conversion rule from the one measure to the other is not defined, and in any case the concept is difficult to use because of the differences in productivity of the individuals or groups concerned, different task types and even different methods of organizing the task.

Conversion Rule: Let us begin with some arbitrary constants to allow us to assume a relationship between the concepts. These should be modified as local need dictates, but the suggested relationships should be clearly stated.

As one basic simplification, I would suggest that the smaller units of time be preferred, since conversion is not necessary. For example, if we used the concept of man-hours consistently (5206 man-hours) rather than the tempting simplification of larger units, we would be less likely to be misunderstood.

Let us suggest that:

6 hours makes a man-day,
5 man-days make a man-week,
48 man-weeks make a man-year,
4 man-weeks make a man-month.

These six programs solve exactly the same problem

TEST	LANGUAGE	HOURS DEVEL-OPMENT TIME	EXECU-TION TIME (sec.)	DEVELOP-MENT COST $	EXECU-TION COST $	ONE USE COST $	MUST RUN THIS NO. OF TIMES TO PAY OFF
1	PROBLEM ORIENTED LANGUAGE Programmer A	3	192	190	28.80	218.80	
2	SAME P. O. L. Programmer B	5	53	200	7.95	207.95	
3	A P L	5.5	4	240	0.44	240.44	
4	ALGOL Programmer C	8.5	1.3	315	0.21	315.21	
5	FORTRAN	20	0.5	600	0.11	600.11	52
6	ALGOL Programmer D	29	5	680	0.75	680.75	

EXPERIMENTAL DATA: – USING PROFESSIONAL PROGRAMMERS
At FEDERAL RESERVE BANK OF NEW YORK
– COMPUTING TREASURY BILL INTEREST RATES
(Newtons approximation)
– DIFFERENT COMPUTERS OF ROUGHLY EQUAL POWER
– PERSONALITY AND ATTITUDE "UNCONTROLLED"

Fig 107. Adapted slightly from: Lawrence H. Cooke, Jr.: Programming
Time vs. Running Time. Datamation, Dec. 1974, pp. 56–58.

which gives us a   30-hour man-week,
                   a 120-hour man-month,
                   a 1440-hour man-year.

Hours are divided into 60 minutes, which are divided into 60 seconds
as usual.

All this is of course an approximation, but at least it indicates the need
for defining these terms when they are used, and will perhaps tempt
those who are not happy with such normalized approximations to make
use of the smaller, but more accurate units of time.

Space metrics

Since all data can ultimately be stored as binary units (bits) and since
binary units can be converted into all other forms of data, we should
use them as our most fundamental unit of measure. They give accuracy
of expression and can be used in any situation.

The bit is the fundamental measure of logical space for data.

It may be convenient to use other units such as <u>words</u> or <u>characters</u> but
the user then has to carefully define the number of bits per word or
character, since these can vary. It is not uncommon for these differences
to be consciously misused to mislead computer equipment buyers into
believing that their storage capacity is greater than it is.

The abbreviations for "thousand" are commonly used in computer
measures. The suggestion that K = 1024 while k = kilo = 1000 has been
proffered, but still leads to some confusion. In cases where accuracy
is of any importance these units should be avoided, and detailed terms
should be used.

Perhaps the Roman "M" should be used for 1000, but this would cause
confusion with the abbreviations for million and mega. Again, the basic
cure is total avoidance of these abbreviations, unless they are defined
locally on the page where they are used.

Compression ratio

The compression ratio is the measure of the degree of compression of data, as expressed by the fraction

$$\frac{\text{Length of original data}}{\text{Length of compressed data}}$$

(Source: Ruth & Kreutzer, "Data Compression for Large Business Files", Datamation, Sept. 1972 pp. 62-66)

A very convenient format of expression is the fraction: for example "The compression ratio did not exceed 2/1."

Diverse metrics

Information

Information is not directly measurable.

Indirectly it may be possible, especially in specific application-oriented circumstances, to construct some indication of the quantity of information by counting instances, subjectively perhaps, of "useful data".

In conventional "information theory" (see for example Systems Engineering Handbook, McGraw-Hill, 1966) information is made measurable in terms of quantities of data.

Information is, it seems, really just that: a measure of data quantity.

But I am unable to see at present how or why to make an indirect measure of information, as it is defined in this text.

By definition, it is an abstract concept which is not actually perceivable, except in some data format.

Information. Concept Comments

Definition: Information is the interpretation of data.

The information may be interpreted by different humans or by different machines in different ways depending on the algorithm used to interpret the data and on the information source which the algorithm may be dependent on (such as tables, files, recollections).

The following factors may be noted:

a. Information itself cannot be "processed", since it is an "interpretation" of data and the interpretation itself becomes data.

b. Information, by itself, is not directly perceivable (nor by inference measurable. Information must always be expressed in some form of data in order to be communicated to any human or machine.

c. The same data may give rise to different information when interpreted by different persons, machines, or algorithms with different reference data (i.e. the data used in the algorithms which attempt to interpret data) or, by implication, at different times by the same people or machines (since their algorithms or reference data may have changed).

d. <u>Different</u> algorithms can result in the <u>same</u> information from the <u>same</u> input data. By implication the different algorithms have different characteristics (such as speed, cost, reliability).

e. <u>"Algorithm design"</u> (= methods design, program design, procedure design, etc.) is the process of selecting a "best known" algorithm according to a balanced set of algorithm characteristics which best satisfy the requirements of the situation in which the algorithm is to perform.

f. The <u>minimum complexity</u> of any algorithm depends on the complexity of the data upon which it is to act and the complexity of the data form in which it is expected to represent its results.

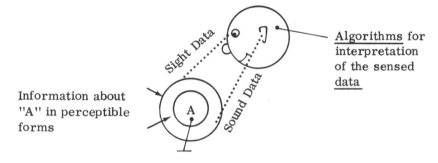

Algorithms for interpretation of the sensed <u>data</u>

Information about "A" in perceptible forms

Sight Data

Sound Data

A

The thing itself ("A") which is imperceptible

Fig 108. <u>Data</u> and <u>information</u> "A" is "the thing 'A' " itself. It cannot be sensed directly. It can only be understood indirectly through data that it generates (image, sound, feel, weight), which we assume reflects "the thing itself". "A" is then the thing which we seek <u>information</u> about through the various <u>data</u> we can obtain about it.

210

Data

a. Data has many possible forms. Thus practical measures will take into account the specific form of the data in question (magnetic, characters, color, etc.)

b. For purposes of automatic data processing, at the current state of the art, there are a few obvious and customary measures of data quantity.

The bit (binary unit): the basic unit of digital data processing systems
The symbol: alphanumeric characters and symbols: in practice these use 7 or 9 bits, including single parity bits.
The "word": an arbitrary machine-oriented unit of data which contains typically 4 to 60 bits.

Bits are a useful unit of measurement when the measure is to be related to machine cost or effort. They are also useful as a common denominator for data quantities.

Symbols are a useful unit of data when measures must relate to human processes.

Notation: (suggested) Db = Data measured in bits. Note: The confusion with "decibels" notation should be resolved by the context. Alternatives: D_b, D_{bit} .

Ds = Data measured in terms of symbols (such as "$%DdAE ¢ 81/2' %?§ & £"). Alternatives: D_s, $D_{symbols}$. Note: The term "characters" or "alphanumeric characters" is often used. This seems too restrictive. On the other hand, it is possible to assert that the term "symbols" has far too wide a range of interpretation. I use the restricted definition: "symbols which can be written by a single depression of a typewriter key".

Data. Concept Comments

Definition: Data are any perceivable things from which information can be derived.

Data are thus everything which humans or machines can sense, and thus perform some algorithm upon, in order to obtain some meaning from them.

Data can include the obvious such as words, numbers, symbols, pictures as well as the less obvious such as color, texture, touch, brightness, electronic or magnetic state.

Thus:

a. A particular set of data is distinguishable from some other set of data, by properties, point in time and location.

b. The same <u>information</u> may be conveyed by many <u>forms</u> of data. This is dependent upon the data interpretation algorithm.

c. There is no theoretical limitation on the number of forms data may take which can result in the <u>same informational interpretation.</u>

d. Each different data form for such information-equivalents has, by implication, different <u>characteristics.</u> (see "information"). For example: space efficiency, speed efficiency, self-correcting redundancy, standard form, interpretation efficiency, etc.

e. A process called "data design" (which is selecting the data form for a specific purpose, according to its characteristics in relation to the objectives of that specific purpose) will have some value as a "discipline", since the resulting product (a specified data form for a specific purpose) will tend to be more effective for its purpose.

DIFFERENT FORMS OF DATA   CAN GIVE THE <u>SAME</u> INFORMATION
(interpretation of data)

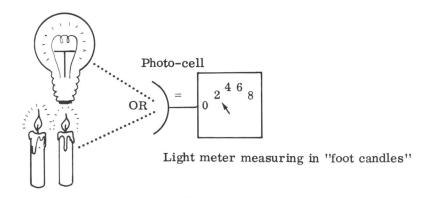

Fig 109.

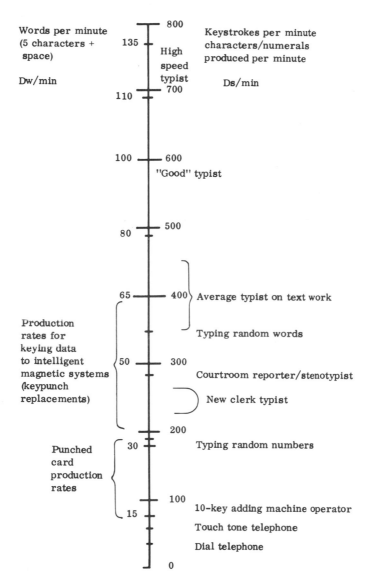

Fig 110. Human data-registration rates for key depression systems for
varied tasks, qualifications, and types of data. Example of use
of the metric concept Ds (data measured in terms of character
symbols). (Adapted from: Marlow et al. :Computerworld: Keypunch
Replacement Handbook. Appendix B, R. Pyes, p. 125.)

Note: the high keying rates for humanized text are due to the fact that the
operator remembers whole words and sentences, rather than having to
think "one abstract symbol at a time". This should be considered when
evaluating the cost and productivity of "humanized codes".

<u>Evolution</u>

M e t r i c

a. Evolution is the design objective of spreading out necessary changes over a relatively long period of time, so that the rate of change as a function of time is low, or at least lower than alternative design possibilities would give.

b. <u>Notation</u>: Ch_s (t)

Degree of change to system "s" during any time interval "t"

The value of Ch varies from 0.0 (no change) to 1.0 (100% change).

c. <u>Measurement</u>: Any convenient indicator of change may be used. There are many possible indicators of relative change and some provide more interesting or more easily available measures than others, for example: number of program instructions changed (in relation to original number); percentage of instruction manuals changed; number of new data elements or changed data elements in a data base.

d. Example: Experience teaches us that organizations appear to have a limited capacity to absorb change successfully.

For this reason, many systems designers plan a gradual introduction of changes, spread over a time period.

E v o l u t i o n – C o n c e p t C o m m e n t s

<u>Definition</u>: Evolution is a designed characteristic of a system development which involves gradual stepwise change.

a. Evolution is a technique for producing the appearance of <u>stability</u> (a system property). But evolution is a process characteristic.

b. A complex system will be most successful if it is implemented in small steps and if each step has a clear measure of successful achievement as well as a "retreat" possibility to a previous successful step upon failure.

c. The advantage is that you cannot have large failures. You have the opportunity of receiving some feedback from the real world before throwing in all resources intended for a system, and you can correct possible design errors before they become costly live systems.

214

d. The disadvantage is that you may sometimes have to wait longer before the whole system is functioning. This is offset by the fact that some results are produced much earlier than they would be if you had to await total system completion. It is also important to distinguish between a date for total system operation and a date for total <u>successful</u> system operation.

e. Many people claim that their system cannot be put into operation gradually. It is all or nothing.

This may conceivably be true in a few cases, such as the transition of motor traffic in Britain from right to left. (They could start off with Northern Ireland first, actually.) I think we shall find that virtually all systems can be fruitfully put-in in more than one step even though some must inevitably take larger steps than others.

Stability

Metric

a. Stability is the system characteristic of remaining relatively unchanged in spite of changes in the system environment. It is therefore measured via a measure of the degree of system change (Ch).

b. <u>Notation</u>: Ch_s (c)

varies from 0.0 (perfect stability: no changes in system "s" are measured as a result of changes "c").

to   1.0 (a maximum of system change in system "s" as a result of changes denoted by "c": in effect the system is replaced by a totally new system).

c. <u>Measurement</u>: The change should reflect the percentage change effected in "s" as a result of system environmental change "c".

In a programmed system, one convenient measurement would be the number of instructions changed, deleted or added to the original instruction logic as a result of "c".

d. <u>Example</u>: 1) A payroll system is designed so that any new payroll or taxation laws have little effect on the larger part of the system. By

215

design and by measured experience

Ch_{pay} (payroll/tax regulations) = 0.05 to 0.01

as measured by number of (% of original programs) changed instructions.

2) On-line interactive terminal operator's language. An on-line terminal system is being designed. It is desired to minimize the need for teaching operators new codes and procedures at the terminal when new systems (booking and credit checking) are added at a later date.

The objective is $Ch_{stage\ 1}$ (booking & checking) = about 0.05, i.e. the maximum <u>change</u> in the first system's terminal input codes and procedures, from the operator's point of view, should not exceed 5% of the total codes and procedures, after the two new systems have been introduced later on.

This will be achieved by making at least a preliminary design of the other two systems' terminal operator languages in order to make sure that they will not make any big changes in the original operator's language necessary.

The function of the measure <u>Ch</u> in this case is to force early clear recognition of the design objective.

Stability - Concept Comments

<u>Definition</u>: Stability is the measure of lack of <u>perceivable</u> change in a system, at a given level of that system, in spite of some occurrence in the system environment which would normally be expected to cause change (see Fig. 111).

a. Stability is a <u>system characteristic</u> which can be <u>consciously designed</u> into the system so that costs and errors due to "changes" are avoided. Since all systems must inevitably undergo some changes, the design objective of stability is to allow those changes to be made but to prevent or reduce effects on selected critical environments.

For example: A system may be designed so that any number of improvements can be made at the computer hardware/software level without changing any of the current procedures of the "users" of the system, for example bank employees and bank customers.

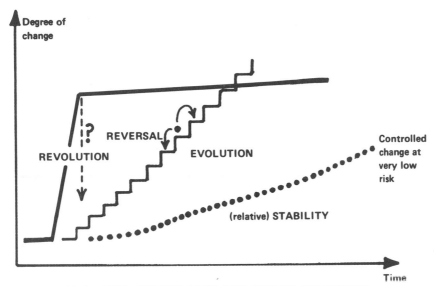

- RISK ESTIMATES ± WORST CASE ARE KEY TO SELECTION OF STEP SIZE

- PETER'S PRINCIPLE: LEVEL OF INCOMPETENCE
                         WHERE IS IT?

- SAVING OF ANALYSIS OF FUTURE REAL WORLD

- SOME RESULTS FASTER

- SOME RESULTS GUARANTEED

Fig 111.

b. <u>Compatibility</u> and <u>portability</u> are specific techniques for achieving stability; so are <u>evolution</u> and <u>reliability</u>.

c. The concept of stability at individual levels of a system has the same <u>usefulness</u> as the concept of keeping all-factors-except-one constant in a scientific experiment. It allows systematic and orderly change of systems where the <u>cause and effect</u> may be more accurately measured without interfering factors, which may cause doubt as to the reason for good or bad results.

Further, the concept of <u>selective stability</u> (and corresponding selective change) allows us to reduce the risk of new system failure because of having "too heavy" a <u>change burden</u> at one time. Systems may be specifically designed to go through a revolution in several phases, where only one level of the system is changed significantly at a time.

Example: first the computer hardware is changed (programs run in hardware compatibility mode), then the programs are changed to a more appropriate language (ASSEMBLY to FORTRAN for example), then the procedures are "improved" and the program functional logic is changed.

Appendixes

APPENDIX A

Cobol program checklist for prompting program inspectors

Cobol program checklist © 1975 by International Business Machines Corporation

During the COBOL inspection the unit being inspected should be examined for the following points.

Error
Type

1. Identification Division

Remarks Paragraph

Does the prose in the REMARKS paragraph function as
a complete prologue for the program?   PR

2. Environment Division

Does each SELECT sentence explicitly define the external
(system-dependent) specifications for the file?   SU

3. Data Division

File Section

Are the File Definitions (FDs) in the same order as their
respective SELECT sentences in the ENVIRONMENT
DIVISION?   DA

Do the record and data item names conform to their
usage?   DA

Does each FD contain comments regarding: DA

Usage of the file (RECORDING MODE, block size,
record length, imbedded keys, etc.)?

Amount of activity (updated how often, used every time
program is run, etc.)?

Interaction with other data items. (Do its records
contain objects of 'Occurs... Depending On' clauses
(ODOs); is the length of its records dependent on an ODO
object elsewhere in the program, etc.?)

222

	Error Type
Is the file SORTed or MERGEd?	EL
Are statistics kept on file activity in a given run or series of runs ?	EL

Working-Storage & Linkage Sections

Do the data item names conform to their usage?	DA
Does each data item (except for elementary items of obvious usage – subscripts, etc.) contain comments regarding:	DA

Characteristics (fixed or variable length, maximum allowable length, etc.)

Interaction with other data items. (Does this data item contain or depend on objects of ODOs, etc. ?)

Area of use in program. (Is it used only in a certain section, or during a range of paragraphs, etc. ?)

Are all data items with any kind of unifying quality placed together according to a particular scheme:	DA

Usage (arithmetic work areas, work areas for file records, etc.)?

Commonality of purpose (everything used to process a particular file, etc.)?

Attributes (message texts, constants, etc.)?

Are all WORKING-STORAGE items that are used as constants designated as such?	DA
Are data items (that are required to be in a particular order) sequenced correctly?	DA

4. Procedure Division

Are block comments included for major functional areas (e. g. , paragraph, SECTION, segment)?	CC
Is the module sufficiently commented (enough detail)?	CC
Are comments accurate and meaningful?	CC
Does the code essentially correspond to the outline of the module documented in the REMARKS paragraph?	LO
Does each paragraph, SECTION, or segment have a homogeneous purpose which justifies and/or necessitates placing all the code together under such a grouping?	MN
Does each performed paragraph or SECTION document the function it accomplishes and what part of the overall logic it represents?	CC
In a segmented program, is it clear why segmentation is necessary?	MN
Is the assignment of paragraphs to, and the arrangement of, the segments such that thrashing between segments is eliminated or held to a minimum?	MN

5. Format

Throughout the module:

Are THEN/ELSE groups aligned?	MN
Are nested IFs indented properly?	MN
Are block comments and remarks effectively positioned?	MN
Are the clauses of complex verbs indented properly and clearly under the verb:	MN
Complex arithmetic (ADD, SUBTRACT, COMPUTE, etc. ?)	

SORT/MERGE?

INVALID KEY/AT END on I-O verbs?

File-names and options on OPEN/CLOSE?

Complex PERFORM?

STRING/UNSTRING ?

SEND/RECEIVE?

SEARCH/SEARCH ALL?

6. Module Logic

Through the module, in verifying that the code matches the design, ensure that the following criteria are met:

ENTRY & EXIT LINKAGE

Is initial entry and final exit correct?	EL
Is each entry point defined correctly?	EL
Is each parameter referenced in an ENTRY statement a 77 or Ø1 item in the LINKAGE SECTION?	EL
Is the usage of STOP RUN/GOBACK/EXIT PROGRAM verbs correct in this module, in the context of the whole of which this module is part?	EL

LOGIC

Has all design been implemented?	LO
Does code do what the design called for; (i. e. is the design translated correctly)?	LO
Is the design correct and complete?	DE

Appropriate number of characters within a field tested or set?	LO
In the PERFORM statement, if loop control is used, is the loop executed the correct number of times and does it access the correct addresses?	LO

Language Usage

Is the optimal verb or set of verbs used?	PU
Is the installation-defined restricted subset of COBOL used throughout the module?	PU
Is attention given to normal 'housekeeping' requirements in COBOL; (e. g. setting the length of a variable-length target field before a MOVE to that field is executed)?	PU

Storage Usage

Is each field to be initialized set correctly?	SU
Before the first use of any field, has it been initialized properly?	SU
Is the correct field specified?	SU
If storage is set and used recursively, is it 'housekept' properly?	SU
Is the field initialized statically (i. e. by means of the VALUE clause on its definition), when it should be dynamically (by assignment), or vice versa?	SU
Is the use of the REDEFINES clause in the data item's definition compatible with all uses of the data item in the code?	SU

Test and Branch

Is correct condition tested (IF X=ON vs. IF X=OFF)?	TB

Is (are) correct variable(s) used for test (IF X=ON vs.
IF Y=ON)?   TB

Is each condition-name, used as a test of a data item,
defined as an 88-level under that data item?   TB

Are null ELSEs included as appropriate?   MN

Is each branch target of a simple GO TO or GO TO ...
DEPENDING ON statement, correct and exercised at
least once?

Is the most frequently exercised test leg of an IF statement
the THEN clause?

Performance

Is logic coded optimally; (i.e. in the fewest and most
efficient statements)?   PE

Has subscripting been used where indexing logic would
be more effective and appropriate, or vice versa?   PE

Have ERROR DECLARATIVEs been coded for files likely
to have recoverable I-O errors?   PE

Maintainability

Are listing controls utilized to enhance readability (e.g.
EJECT, SKIPx)?   MN

Are paragraph and SECTION names consistent with the
logical significance of the code?   MN

Is each PERFORMed paragraph terminated with an EXIT
paragraph?   MN

Linkage Requirements

For each external call to another module: EL

    Are all required parameters passed to each called
    module?

Are the parameter values passed set correctly?

Upon final exit from this module, are all files closed?

Copy Facility Usage

Is every data item definition and processing paragraph, standardized for the installation, generated in the module via the <u>COPY</u> facility? OT

Is there a sound reason why the <u>REPLACE</u> option of the <u>COPY</u> statement is utilized to change any of the names of data items in the <u>COPY</u>'d code? OT

Note:

This checklist is not an exhaustive set of prompting questions; however, it is considered to be representative of and applicable to most COBOL programs.

APPENDIX B

Process description of test inspection including some associated forms

Process description of test inspection and associated forms

(From pp. 9-32 of Rodney R. Larson, TEST PLAN AND TEST CASE
INSPECTION SPECIFICATION: TR 21.586, April 4 1975)

I. IT-1 PROCESS

The IT-1 will consist of five stages (presupposes that I-0 was attended
by all participants).

1. Planning

2. Preparation for inspection

3. Inspection

4. Rework

5. Follow-up

The planning activity is to identify the material and personnel required,
and to schedule the time and place of the inspection.

Preparation is the period of time prior to the inspection in which the
participants will review the Test Plan for a particular function against
the Final Programming Functional Specs (FPFS) and other High Level
Design documentation.

The inspection is a formal method of examining the Test Plan, the
purpose being to assure the completeness and accuracy of the Test Plan.

Rework is the period of time following the inspection in which errors or
omissions found during the inspection will be fixed.

Follow-up is the process to insure that all problems found have been
correctly fixed in the Test Plan.

II. PARTICIPANTS

Moderator

An independent, impartial individual who coordinates the planning,
preparation, conduct of inspection and follow-up activities of the IT-1.
During the inspection he assures that the inspection is efficiently conducted in terms of resource utilization and achieving the maximum effort
toward detecting problems.

Functional Tester

Person responsible for providing the Test Plan input for the function being tested. Will present the Test Plan to the rest of the participants.

Functional Designer

The designer of the function being tested. Should verify that the function as designed is being comprehensively exercised in an appropriate environment. (He is the Key Inspector. It is assumed he is the most knowledgeable and, hence, an "authority" on the function being tested.)

Inspectors (Design and/or Development)

Individuals responsible for the implementation of this function into their subcomponent. Should verify that the significant code changes to their subcomponent (particularly interface hits) will be exercised.

NOTE: If the FV Test Plan addresses several functions within a component, there will be one IT-1 for each function. In such cases, it is worthwhile to have one of the participants attend all the inspections in order to provide continuity of testing between functions. Frequently, Test Cases designed to exercise one function can be slightly modified to accommodate other functions as well.

III. PREPARATION

Each participant must prepare for the IT-1 by reading the Test Plan and the accompanying materials distributed prior to the IT-1. The technical content of the materials should be compared for discrepancies as they are read.

Materials

1. Test Plan

    For purposes of this report, it is assumed the Test Plan will minimally contain the following information:

    a. A general test philosophy or strategy.

b. Functional description of what is being tested.

c. A representation of functional coverage (i. e. , matrix, cause and effect graph, family tree, etc.)

d. A description of what each Test Case will test and how it will be accomplished.

e. Testing dependencies (build requirements, hardware/simulator needs, etc.)

f. Entrance and Exit Criteria.

2. FPFS and Other Available High Level Designs.

Each participant should verify that the function (and the significant impact to the code) is being properly exercised, based on the Test Plan description.

Any discrepancies or errors found during preparation should be noted for attention at the IT-1.

IV. INSPECTION

The inspection will consist of reviewing the planned testing activity, as documented in the Test Plan, against the provided design materials. Types of questions that should be addressed are:

1. Is the description of the function being tested, as documented in the Test Plan, complete and accurate ?

2. Are sufficient mainline and variations executed to provide confidence that the function being tested operates correctly ?

3. Is the testing approach feasible ?

4. Is all the new and/or changed User Interface exercised ?

5. Sufficient number of defaults exercised ?

6. * Are messages verified ?

7. * Error paths exercised ?

8. * Return codes generated ?

9. Are sufficient and proper tests identified to reverify previously tested related functions (Regression Test Cases) ?

---

* May not be necessary if verified through other testing activities.

10. Are there Simulator and Hardware dependencies that are not addressed?

11. Driver support available to test function as specified (scaffolding required)?

12. Test Plan Entrance and Exit criteria realistic?

13. Are there any outstanding Design changes to be made which will invalidate the completeness of the Test Plan?

If, during the Inspection, areas are identified that require testing which are not addressed by the FV Test Plan, do not attempt to identify what error detection operation is the appropriate one (i. e., Unit Test, FV, Component Test, etc.). Record the problem, continue with the Inspection, and resolve off-line what activity is responsible for testing that area. If it is determined that FV is the appropriate activity, the Moderator must verify that the FV Test Plan is updated to include such testing.

V. REWORK

Rework identified at the IT-1 will be recorded by the Moderator (see attachments I and II for IT-1 forms). It will be the Tester's responsibility to correct the problems found during the IT-1 and update the appropriate documentation.

VI. FOLLOW-UP

It will be the Moderator's responsibility to see that all problems resulting from the IT-1 are documented and verify that fixes have been implemented prior to IT-1 exit.

Inspection report data is put into a data base for analyzing and feedback to the parties concerned to improve future efforts.

IT-2 DESCRIPTION

IT-2 Inspections are conducted against a clean compilation of each Test
Case, using the FV Test Plan as the reference document. If the Test
Case is common to more than one system, listings for each system
being tested should be available at the inspection. The primary objective
of the IT-2 is to verify the following:

1. The Test Case causes to be executed those variations as described
   in the FV Test Plan.

2. The Test Case Prologue provides a complete and accurate description
   of its purpose, explicit instructions on its execution, and identifies
   all expected results.

3. The Test Case Code will execute correctly (i. e. no bugs).

I. IT-2 PROCESS

The IT-2 consists of the same five stages as identified for an IT-1:
Planning, Preparation, Inspection, Rework, and Follow-Up.

Planning is the same as identified for an IT-1.

Preparation is the period of time prior to the Inspection in which the
participants will review clean compilations of the Test Case against
the FV Test Plan.

The Inspection consist of a meeting of the participants to formally
examine each Test Case. Purpose is to assure the Test Cases correctly
execute all the variations called for in the Test Plan.

Rework and Follow-Up stages are the same as identified for an IT-1.

II. PARTICIPANTS

Moderator

(Same description applies as stated for the IT-1)

Tester

Person responsible for the Test Case being inspected.

Inspector 1

This inspector should be an individual experienced in <u>running</u> FV Test Cases. He should be primarily concerned that the prologue identifies Test Case dependencies, provides the necessary information for the operator, and that all the operator's needs are provided for by the Test Case code; (i.e., dumps, messages, timer loops, etc.).

Inspector 2

This inspector should be an individual experienced in <u>coding</u> user-type programs for this component. He should be primarily concerned with the correct coding of the Test Case.

III. PREPARATION

Each participant <u>must prepare</u> for the IT-2 by reviewing the Test Case listing and comparing it with its description as defined in the FV Test Plan.

Materials

1. Test Case Listing

   For purposes of this report, it is assumed the Test Case prologue will minimally contain the following information:

   a. A description and purpose of the Test Case

   b. SYSGEN and set-up requirements

   c. Operator instructions for running the Test Case

   d. Normal and abnormal completion messages

   e. Dependencies required by this Test Case (i.e., Simulator, Hardware, test macros, etc.)

   f. Name of owner of the Test Case.

2. Those sections of the FV Test Plan necessary to define this Test Case.

3. A copy of the FPFS should be available at the Inspection for reference.

IV. INSPECTION

The Inspection will consist of the Tester leading the team through the Test Case prologue and code. Type of questions to be addressed are:

Prologue

1. Is the description of the purpose of this Test Case complete and accurate?

2. Are the Operator instructions explicit and clear for ease of Test Case execution?

3. Are all dependencies identified?

4. Are all normal and abnormal completion messages identified?

5. Are set-up requirements explicit and complete?

6. Owner of the Test Case identified?

7. Are there "progress" messages identified that will notify the Operator when significant parts of the Test Case are being executed?

Code

1. Does the Test Case logic follow its description as defined in the FV Test Plan?

2. Are the appropriate conditions established to test the intended variations?

3. Is the test for successful completion correct?

4. Are initial Declares, Respecifies, and Includes complete and correct?

5. Is Entry and Exit linkage correct?

6. Are macros issued properly?

7. Appropriate Return and Feedback codes properly verified?

8. Are the messages as identified in the prologue issued in the Code?

NOTE: If Test Case is written for more than one system (like VS-1 and VS-2) and using higher level language (like PLS), diversify the listings being used (e.g., have one inspector use PLS/VS-1 and another inspector use BAL/VS-2.)

V. REWORK

Rework identified at the IT-2 will be recorded by the Moderator (see attachments A and C for IT-2 forms). It will be the Tester's responsibility to correct the problems found during the IT-2 before providing the Test Case for execution.

VI. FOLLOW-UP

It will be the Moderator's responsibility to see that all problems resulting from the IT-2 are documented and verify that fixes have been implemented prior to IT-2 exit.

Inspection report data is put into a data base for analyzing and feedback to the concerned parties to help improve future efforts.

ATTACHMENT I

INSPECTION REPORT

TO: DATE:_____

SUBJECT:

1. An _____[(1)] Inspection was held on_____[(2)].

    The detailed results of the Inspection are contained on the
    attached forms.

    A.   SYSTEMS AFFECTED:_____[(3)]

    B.   COMPONENT:_____[(4)]

    C.   FUNCTION:_____[(5)]

    D.   RELEASE:_____[(6)]

    E.   BUILD INCREMENT:_____[(7)]

2. Results of the Inspection are summarized below:

    A.   INSPECTION LENGTH:_____Hours [(8)]

    B.   NUMBER OF PROBLEMS FOUND:

          MAJOR:_____[(9)]

          MINOR:_____[(10)]

          TOTAL:_____[(11)]

    C.   TOTAL ESTIMATED REWORK HOURS:_____[(12)]

    D.   TOTAL LINES OF CODE INSPECTED:_____[(13)]

    E.   REINSPECTION REQUIRED? _____
          (See attachment for MOD/MAC)[(14)]

                    SIGNED BY:_____[(15)]

INSTRUCTIONS FOR FILLING OUT INSPECTION REPORT

The inspection report is the cover sheet for all inspections. Its purpose is to concisely summarize the inspection results.

Listed below is an explanation of each entry:

1. Type of inspection held: IT-1 or IT-2

2. Date of the inspection

3. System or systems affected

4. Name of component

5. Name of function

6. Release the inspection material is targeted for

7. Driver build applicable for the material being tested

8. Length of inspection in hours

9. Total number of Major* problems found in the inspection

10. Total number of Minor* problems found in the inspection

11. Total of Majors and Minors

12. Number of hours required to fix all recorded problems

13. Total lines of code inspected (N/A for IT-1 since dealing with a "function" not LOC)

14. If a reinspection is necessary indicate "yes"; otherwise "no". Moderator determines necessity of reinspection based on number and/or magnitude of problems.

15. Moderator's signature

---

* Definition of Major and Minor problems is contained on IT-1 and IT-2 Inspection Report Forms.

ATTACHMENT II
TEST PLAN INSPECTION REPORT (IT-1)

DATE_____
(1)

FUNCTION:_____

PROBLEM TYPE:(2)	MAJOR			MINOR *			TOTAL
	M	W	E	M	W	E	
FD: Functional Description							
TP: Test Procedure							
TS: Test Strategy							
FM: Family Tree/Matrix							
TD: Test Case Description							
RT: Regression Tests							
BR: Build Requirements							
SH: Simulator/Hardware							
DR: FV Driver							
OT: Other							
Subtotal:							
TOTAL:							

MODERATOR:_____ (3)   INSPECTORS:_____ (7)

FUNCTIONAL
TESTER:_____ (4)   _____

FUNCTIONAL
DESIGNER:_____ (5)   _____

INSPECTION TIME (P. HRS.):___ (6) RE-INSPECTION REQUIRED___ (Y or N) (8)

* (Typos, editorial changes, etc.)
(M=Missing, W=Wrong, E=Extra)

INSTRUCTIONS FOR FILLING OUT TEST PLAN INSPECTION REPORT (IT-1)

(1) Name of function being inspected

(2) Summarize in the appropriate box the number of problems found in that category (i.e., if four Minor problems were found in the Functional Description [three wrong and one missing], a "1" would appear opposite "FD" under "MINOR", "M" and a "3" under "MINOR, "W".)

A complete description of each problem would be recorded and attached to the report. In this case, one problem would be identified as MIN/FD/M and three as MIN/FD/W. Each would be followed by a detailed description of the problem.

(3) Name of Moderator for this inspection

(4) Name of Functional Tester

(5) Name of Functional Designer

(6) Number of people hours expended in the inspection

(7) Names of other Inspectors

(8) If reinspection required enter "Y"; otherwise "N"

ATTACHMENT III

TEST CASE INSPECTION (IT-2)

DATE_____

TEST CASE:_____ (1) FUNCTION:_____ (2)

PROBLEM TYPE: (3)

	MAJOR*			MINOR			TOTAL
	M	W	E	M	W	E	

DR: Description_____

OI: Operator Instructions_____

MG: Messages_____

SG: SYSGEN Requirements_____

DP: Dependencies_____

LO: Logic_____

RU: Register Usage_____

MU: Macro Usage_____

PU: PL/S or BAL Usage_____

IR: Interface_____

CC: Code Comments_____

OT: Other_____

Subtotal:

TOTAL: _____ _____ _____

MODERATOR:_____ (4) INSPECTORS:_____ (8)

TESTER:_____ (5) _____

INSPECTION TIME (P. HRS.):_____ (6) REWORK HRS:_____ (9)

RE-INSPECTION REQUIRED?_____ (7) (Y or N) LOC:_____ (10)

* (Problems that result in erronous execution of Test Case)
  (M=Missing, W=Wrong, E=Extra)

INSTRUCTIONS FOR FILLING OUT TEST CASE INSPECTION (IT-2)

One form is completed for each Test Case examined in the inspection.

(1) Name of Test Case being inspected

(2) Name of Function Test Case was written to exercise

(3) Summarize in the appropriate box the number of problems found in that category. Attach a description of each problem found in this Test Case and identify by problem type (e.g., MAJ/MG/W, etc.)

(4) Name of Moderator for this inspection

(5) Name of Tester responsible for this Test Case

(6) Number of people hours expended in the inspection

(7) If reinspection required, enter "Y"; otherwise "N"

(8) Names of Inspectors at the inspection

(9) Number of hours required to correct all recorded problems for this Test Case.

(10) Number of lines of code (LOC) inspected in this Test Case (N/A for script T/C)

APPENDIX C

A sample software /services/ software conversion and hardware Mecca model

Summary of elements and weights for MAIN COMPUTER

	Levels: 1	2	3	4	5	% Weights Groups	Elementary
1. SUPPLIER	30						
11. Support during implementation		16				4.8	
110 Support in syst. an. & design			45				2.26
111 Support in programming			20				0.96
112 Support in operations of hardware			15				0.72
113 Test time before delivery			20				0.96
12. Support after implementation		3					0.90
13. Support before contract		5				1.5	
130 Quality of proposal			65				0.98
131 Quality & availability of experts (abroad)			15				0.22
132 Quality & availability of experts (Scandinavia)			20				0.30
14. References/experience		12				3.6	
140 References & experience in industry			50				1.80
141 Scandinavia base of experience			25				0.90
142 Ref. & exp. in on-line prod. control			25				0.90
15. Education/training		16				4.8	
150 Main processor programming			16				0.77
152 Supervisory program			20				0.96
153 File-oriented software			15				0.72
154 Other software			8				0.38
155 General courses			7				0.34
157 Educ./training of operators			15				0.72
158 Educ./training of maint. personnel			7				0.34
159 Training periods at user sites			12				0.58

246

MAIN COMPUTER

			% Weights				
Levels:	1	2	3	4	5	Group	Elementary
16. The contract	33					9.9	
160 Guarantees of hardware			10				0.99
161 Guarantees of software			10				0.99
162 Guarantees of support/education documentation			10				0.99
163 Guarantees of throughput/acceptance tests			10				0.99
164 Reduction of rental if guarantees not met			20				1.98
165 Guarantees of right delivery			10				0.99
166 Guarantees of back-up			10				0.99
167 Degree of correspondence with state contract			20				1.98
17. Hardware maintenance	10					3.0	
170 Spare parts inventory (where/how)							
171 Representation							
172 Quality of maintenance							
173 Extra payments							
174 Participation in hardware maintenance							
18. Software maintenance	5					1.5	
180 Organization			60				0.90
181 Representation			30				0.45
182 Quality			10				0.15

Originally reproduced in an article by Tom Scharf Gilb in IAG Quarterly Journal Vol. 3, 1969.

MAIN COMPUTER

	% Weights						
Levels:	1	2	3	4	5	Group	Elementary
2. HARDWARE	20						
21. Central Processing Unit		50				10.0	
210 Processor			35			3.5	
2100 Commercial Gibson mix				30			1.05
2101 Gibson III mix				10			0.35
2102 Processor features				50		1.75	
21020 Index registers					25		0.44
21021 Memory protect					30		0.52
21022 Real time clock					30		0.52
21023 Decimal arithmetics					5		0.09
21024 Interrupt system					10		0.18
2103 Special instructions				5			0.18
2104 Upgrading				5			0.18
211 High speed memory			35			3.5	
2110 Capacity				50			1.75
2111 Cycle time				25			0.88
2112 Expandability				25			0.88
212 I/O Channel system			30			3.0	
2120 Low speed channels				20			0.60
2121 High speed channels				30			0.90
2122 Simultaneity				50			1.50
22. Files		30				6.0	
220 Direct access files			80			4.8	
2200 On-line capacity				25			1.20
2201 Time for accessing				25			1.20

MAIN COMPUTER

	Levels: 1	2	3	4	5	% Weights Group	Elementary
2202 Expandability				10			0.48
2203 Hardware checks				15			0.72
2204 Removable media				10			0.48
2205 Flexibility in packing				10			0.48
2206 Dual-channel controller				5			0.24
221 Magnetic tape			20			1.2	
2210 Effective transfer rate				20			0.24
2211 Capacity				20			0.24
2212 USASI standard code possible				10			0.12
2213 Compatibility with G 30 tapes				15			0.18
2214 Hardware checks & software actions				15			0.18
2215 Read reverse				15			0.18
2216 Dual channel simultaneity				5			0.06
23. Input/Output equipment	15					3.0	
230 Card reader			15				0.45
231 Paper tape reader			30				0.90
232 Line printer			50				1.50
233 Console typewriter			5				0.15
24. Link between computers	5						1.00
25. Terminals	0						
250 Key-in units							
251 Teletypes							
2510 Printing speed							
2511 Code							

249

MAIN COMPUTER

	% Weights						
Levels:	1	2	3	4	5	Group	Elementary

2512 Supporting software available
2513 Reliability
2514 Technical features
2515 Error checking & corrections
2516 Operating features
2517 Paper tape input/output
252 Alphanumeric displays
2520 Printing speed
2521 Code
2522 Supp. software available
2523 Reliability
2524 Technical features
2525 Error checking & corrections
2526 Ergonomic factors
2527 Editing capabilities
2528 Hard copy options
253 Automatic read-off units
254 Special displays

MAIN COMPUTER

							% Weight	
	Levels:	1	2	3	4	5	Group	Elementary
3. SOFTWARE		20						
31. Supervisory Program			30				6.0	
310 Core requirements, modularity				15				0.90
311 MOP/time-sharing				15				0.90
312 Multiprogramming features				15				0.90
313 Handling & scheduling features				15			0.9	
3130 Input/output handling					30			0.27
3131 Comm. line & terminal handling					10			0.09
3132 Seek on EDS arms					10			0.09
3133 Time-initiated actions handling					10			0.09
3134 Interrupt handling					10			0.09
3135 Comm. between computers					20			0.18
3136 Budgeting system					10			0.09
314 Allocation of core storage				15				0.90
315 Operation features				10				0.60
316 Security features				15				0.90
317 Disc/drum requirements				0				
32. Application Programs & Packages			20				4.0	
320 Industry specials				20				0.80
321 General packages				50				2.00
322 On-line support programs				10				0.40
323 Utility programs				20				0.80
33. Programming languages			25				5.0	
330 FORTRAN				40			2.0	

MAIN COMPUTER

	Levels: 1	2	3	4	5	Group	Elementary
				% Weight			
3300 Compiler				30			0.60
3301 Facilities				30			0.60
3302 Documentation				20			0.40
3303 Relation to USASI standards				20			0.40
331 COBOL			30			1.5	
3310 Compiler				30			0.45
3311 Facilities				30			0.45
3312 Documentation				20			0.30
3313 Relation to USASI standards				20			0.30
332 Assembler			20			1.0	
333 Other languages			10			0.5	
34. File-oriented software facilities	25					5.0	
340 Basic file-oriented facilities			85			4.25	
3400 Neutrality (device)				20			0.85
3401 Security				20			0.85
3402 Protection				15			0.64
3403 Record organization				10			0.43
3404 Directory				20			0.85
3405 Access methods				15			0.64
341 Advanced (data-base) facilities			10				0.50
342 Source and object program file facilities			5				0.25

252

MAIN COMPUTER

	Levels:	1	2	3	4	5	Group	Elementary
							% Weight	
4. PERFORMANCE		20						
41. Load factors			30				6.0	
410 Core storage				25				1.50
411 Processor				20				1.20
412 Channel system				15				0.90
413 Access mechanisms				20				1.20
414 Link between computers				20				1.20
42. Response times for terminals			0					
43. Throughput			25				5.0	
44. Back-up efficiency/reliability			25				5.0	
45. Benchmark results			20				4.0	
450 FORTRAN				50				2.0
451 COBOL				50				2.0

253

MAIN COMPUTER

	1	2	3	4	5	Group	Elementary
Levels:						% Weight	
5. CONVERSION FROM GAMMA 30	10						
51. Translation of source programs		40				4.0	
510 Translator program			30				1.20
511 Conversion of files			20				0.80
512 Manual work with translation			20				0.80
513 Supplier assistance			20				0.80
514 Gamma 30 library			10				0.40
52. Emulation/simulation		30					3.0
53. Benchmark tests		30				3.0	
530 Translation			50			1.5	
5300 Quality of results				30			0.45
5301 Speed				35			0.53
5302 Suppliers assistance				35			0.53
531 Emulation/simulation			50			1.5	
5310 Quality of results				25			0.38
5311 Speed				40			0.60
5312 Suppliers assistance				35			0.52

Number of elementary elements = 147

Average weight per el. element = 0.7%

254

APPENDIX D

An example of notation of software characteristics on the
Mecca element data collection form

System : 314 Superv. Allocation of "core"	project no. : DLNJ
Subsystem : and FILE space.	chapter/sect. : DATA
Prev. issue: 31 Supervisory Program	page : 314
written by : TSS	issued : 23.7
approved by: All Suppliers	

Config. A   Decision documentation[1]

ICL
George 3

No fixed partitions. Core cleanup as needed to reserve space. A program may request additional core during execution or release core. All programs get CONTIGUOUS space (even when additional space allocated)

           Manual G3-237 p. 45 to 48

PERIPHERAL & FILE ALLOCATION: References by "class" of device: Operator can remove a device from scheduling:

Points

8

We can define any group of devices and assign them a generic name: This is only valid for one given program (?) Permanent Private Files demand exact track locations (G 2 ? ?) You can allocate several files on the same cylinder (= split cylinder)

           Manual G3-238 p. 45, 67-69

Config. B   Decision documentation[1]

etc. for other suppliers or other configurations of same supplier.

Points

Config. C   Decision documentation[1]

Acknowledgements

It is obvious that I am deeply indebted to a large number of colleagues for the development of the ideas expressed here, for confirmation that others think along the same lines, and for being able to report the state of this art.

I have made every effort to properly credit the companies and individuals involved, or to preserve their anonymity as appropriate. I have also tried to ask permission to reproduce the many illustrations taken from the works of others, who have been generous in their approval and additional help. I especially wish to thank TRW-Systems and Barry Boehm for providing me with an exceptional volume and quality of material on this particular subject. Truly TRW-Systems must be rated as the pioneer in the broad-based development of software metrics.

I am particularly indebted to Mike Fagan of IBM for his development of the inspection concept and for his personal effort to keep me informed of the results of further work in this area.

A large number of other professionals from all over the world have taken the time to contribute documentation and experiences. Sometimes the debates and professional exchanges carried on by post with people like G. Weinberg, G. Myers, Michael Jackson, Tony Hoare, Jean-Claude Rault and David Gries have contributed to my understanding of the need for a book like this.

The entire first part of this book is the result of a suggestion by my publisher's reader who, when reading the second half of the book (which was, at one point, all I had thought to present), remarked that the concepts of measurement were indeed interesting, but he did not see how they could be implemented in practice. Part I is my answer. And I will admit that it was a much-needed supplement.

Alison Olsen must be credited with a remarkable ability to improve the clarity of the language used in the manuscript. I found it surprising how often she could point out to me passages which even I could not understand, and how often she was able to suggest what I meant to say before I happened upon it myself. Whatever unclear parts remain are surely only due to the fact that she is convinced that it is normal computer terminology and

257

I am blind to the lack of clarity. Forgive me, readers, because I am too weary to attempt the complete rewrite which would ease the pain of reading. It seems better to get this "program" on the air and to improve its structure when it proves its viability.

Finally I must thank my seminar participants in four continents for letting me try out my teaching on them, and for giving me so much useful criticism and comments. And then, of course, I wish to thank everybody who thinks I forgot to thank them!

References

Abernathy et al., "Survey of Design Goals for Operating Systems," in
Operating Systems Review (ACM SIGOPS), July 1973, Jan 1974
Georgia Inst. of Tech. Report GITIS-72-04. These authors
appreciate the necessity of describing software in terms of a
large number of multidimensional attributes of the kind discussed in the present text. They also appreciate the fact that there
is a trade-off conflict between these attributes. There is, however no attempt to quantify or actually measure these concepts.
This results in highly undefined concepts of quality and degree
of quality, and in a highly muddled paper which spreads unsound
methodology. The paper might have some interest as a student
exercise, for criticism and rewriting in terms of quantifiable
and measurable software goals.

Andersen, I et al., PLIX - Program Readability Index, Report 75/1
(Danish version; an English translation is being prepared),
Datalogical Institute, University of Copenhagen. This report
describes a series of experiments to correlate human program
readability judgement (on a numeric scale) with a program
for doing the same evaluation.

Belady, L.A. and Lehman, M.M., Programming System Dynamics or
The Meta-Dynamics of Systems in Maintenance and Growth.
IBM RC 35461, Sept. 17, 1971, IBM T.J. Watson Research
Center.
This is mainly concerned with a model for exponential main-
tenance effort growth due to increasing complexity of software
systems. A number of parameters used in building the model
suggest some software metrics.

BERNACCHI-73-20889: Bernacchi, Richard L. and Larsen, Gerald H.
Data Processing Contracts and the Law. $ 25, 715 pp, 1974,
Little Brown and Co., Boston. This is a broadly based and
very well presented book on formal EDP hardware and software
and services specification.

Boehm, B. W. et al., " Structured Programming: A Quantitative Assessment", in Computer (IEEE), June 1975. This and several other

papers in this special issue devoted to the Lake Arrowhead
Structured Programming Conference, report interesting and
important attempts to quantify practical experience with several
new programming methods. It is worthy of note that some care
was taken to make notes about the environment surrounding the
measures so that the reader could better judge the factors involved before accepting comparative figures or cause-effect
explanations. Considering the conference environment in which
these data were collected, I think this is an excellent example
of the practical use of metrics to give more useful information
on software techniques than is usual at present.

DEMARS-73: Demars, G., Girard, E. and Rault, J-C. (of Thomson-CSF,
Paris) "APL in a Two-Step Programming Technique for
Developing Complex Programs", pp. 83-90, APL Congress,
Copenhagen 1973 (August). This paper describes the use of
APL and FORTRAN in parallel for producing dual code. Errors
are found by differences in outputs.

DICKSON-1972: Dickson et al: "Quantitative Analysis of Software
Reliability", pp. 148-157, Proceedings of 1972 Reliability and
Maintainability Symposium, Annals of Assurance Science, IEEE
Catalog Number 72CHO577-7R.

Dujmović, J., "Evaluation, Comparison and Optimation of Digital Computers
Using the Theory of Complex Criteria". Resumé of paper sub-
mitted to Eurocomp-76 received in private communication from
author: University of Belgrade, Department of Electrical
Engineering, P O Box 816, YU-11001 Belgrade, Jugoslavia.
This paper is based on a doctoral thesis work which dealt with
the MECCA-type methods. An essentially identical method
called Mixed Averaging by Levels (MAL) is described and an
example of the application of the method to the evaluation of
hybrid computer hardware is given.

FAGAN-21572: Fagan, Michael E., <u>Design and Code Inspections and
Process Control in the Development of Programs.</u> IBM Technical
Report TR 21. 572. Dec 17 1974. 31 pp.
Author's present address (751104) IBM Corp., Dept D14, 706-2,
P. O. Box 390, Poughkeepsie, N.Y., USA. This report is
extensively quoted from in the present text. An updated version
is due in 1976. Request TR 00.2763 of June 10, 1976.

FARR-65: Farr, L. and Zagorski, H.J., "Quantitative Analysis of
Programming Cost Factors: A Progress Report", in Frielink,

A. B. (ed.), Economics of Automatic Data Processing. ICC
Symposium Proceedings 1965 Rome, Published by North-Holland,
Amsterdam 1965, 384 pp.
This certainly represents an admirable pioneer work in the
software metrics field. Particularly interesting is the attempt
to measure logical complexity by counting logical branches.
The main results are reproduced in the present work.

FISCHLER-75: Fischler et al., "Distinct Software: An Approach to Reliable
Computing." Lockheed Research, 3251 Hanover, Palo Alto 94304
CA, USA. Included in 1975 Japan-USA Computer Conference
Proceedings.
These authors developed the concept of "distinctness" (see
present text) and have made the most thorough exploration of
the dual and parallel-operating programs which I have seen to
date.

FISCHLER-74: Fischler, M. A., Firschein, O., Drew, D. L. Distinct
Software: An Approach to Reliable Computing, Unpublished
stenciled paper Nov 1974, Lockheed Missles, 3251 Hanover
St, Palo Alto, CA94304. This paper is similar to the published
ref. FISCHLER-75 but it contains details and results of several
experiments conducted using dual code.

FRAGOLA-1973: Fragola, J. R. and Spahn, J. F. (Grumman Aerospace,
Bethpage, NY) "The Software Error Effects Analysis: A
Qualitative Design Tool," in 1973 IEEE Symp. on Comp. Softw.
Rel., IEEE Cat No. 73CH0741-9CSR. This paper shows the use
of a quantitative (1 to 7) scale for error seriousness.

Freilink (ed.), Economics of ADP. North-Holland, 1965, See esp.
paper by Farr and Zagorski.

GILB-2/69: Scharf, Tom (Gilb), "Weighted Ranking by Levels" (an early
term for what we now call MECCA). IAG Journal, no. 2, 1969,
pp. 7-23.

GILB-3/69: Scharf, Tom (Gilb), "Weighted Ranking by Levels Computer
Evaluation Method - One Year of Experience". IAG Journal 3,
1969. pages 71-91. See reference GILB-2/69.
References to other literature about the method will be found
here. Copies of these articles and some other considerations
about the method are included in Gilb, T. Reliable Data Systems,
1971, Universitetsforlaget, Box 293, Blindern, Oslo 3. This is
a photocopy of a preliminary manuscript and is obsolete, except
for these references.

GILB-720906: Gilb, T., "Software Portability", in <u>Management Informatics</u> (IAG), Dec. 1974 p. 294, in <u>Data Management</u> (DPMA, USA), June 1974, and a different but related note in <u>Computerworld</u> Sept. 6, 1972, p. 10. These are all popular articles trying to show that the concept of program portability has a metric, and is measurable in practice.

GILB-750401: Gilb, T., "Bebugging" in <u>IAG Communications</u> 1/75 and in (IAG) <u>Management Datamatics,</u> April 1975.
This is a short, popular description of the artificial bug insemination method.

GILB-750617: Gilb, T. "Software Metrics" (identical with 750701). <u>Data (Copenhagen)</u> no. 6, June 1975, pages 63-65.

GILB-750701: Gilb, T. "Software Metrics, The Emerging Technology". <u>Data Management (USA)</u>, July 1975, pages 34-37. Almost a summary of the first part of this book.

GILB-CACM-7502: Gilb, T., "When are we going to structure the knowledge about programming techniques", letter in ACM <u>Communications,</u> March 1975, p. 187-8. An appeal to stop talking and start quantifying the effects of structured programming.

GILB-CTC-74: Gilb, Tom, <u>Controlling the Computer</u>. Studentlitteratur AB, Lund, Sweden, ISBN 91-44-10791-9, 1974, 79 pages, softcover. Also published in several other languages including German ("Kontrolle der EDV", <u>ONLINE magazine,</u> Köln), Swedish (Att <u>Tämja en Dator,</u> Studentlitteratur ISBN 91-44-10781-1) and Dutch (<u>Blijf uw Computer de Baas</u>!, Metacon BV, Bortesiusl. 1 Naarden, 1975). The book is written for executives who are not computer specialists. A large part of the book is devoted to the MECCA method and to software metrics (at the executive level). Readers might find this tool useful for getting support from their bosses for increased formalization in software measures.

GILB-DAT-7410: Gilb, T., "Parallel Programming", <u>Datamation,</u> Oct. 1974, pp. 160-61.
This is a short popularized overview of the dual coding method. It is probably the earliest widely circulated mention of the topic.

GILB-DBS-73: Gilb, T., "Data Base Software - A Sceptical Viewpoint and Some Alternatives". Paper in <u>Infotech State of the Art Report on Data Base Management.</u> ISBN 8553-9140-5, July 1973,

pp. 489–520. Partially reproduced in <u>Management Informatics</u> Oct. 1973, pp. 227–234.
This article makes use of multidimensional metric concepts for analysis of attributes of large generalized data base management systems. One of the alternatives suggested (also in <u>IAG Communications</u> 3/4 1972, pp. 21–24) the Data Optimization Language, describes a hypothetical system attribute specification language for automatic system design and self-adjustment.

GILB-MD-1/75: Gilb, T., "Maintainability", in <u>Management Datamatics,</u> 1/75. An IAG publication. A popular introduction to the maintainability metric.

GILB-RDS-71: Gilb, T., <u>Reliable Data Systems: Design and Management.</u> (Preliminary, raw unedited manuscript edition), Universitetsforlaget ISBN 82 00 04566. 1971 428 pp., $15. See especially 8/5 Measures, 3/6. Now out of date, replaced by GILB-READ-74. This preliminary work contains some of the original ideas which led to the writing of the present manuscript.

GILB-RE-76, Gilb, T., <u>Data Engineering</u>, Studentlitteratur 1976, Samsom, Holland (Dutch Translation) 1976.
This is a completely rewritten and updated replacement for GILB-READ-74. It does not contain any metrics, but it is more detailed in the design of measuring devices in records and files.

GILB-READ-74: Gilb, T., <u>Reliable EDP Application Design.</u> Studentlitteratur, 1973, ISBN 91-44-06091-2, Petrocelli, N.Y., 1974, Müllerverlag Köln (German trans.) 1974. The last chapter "Reliability Datametrics" is an early published collection of 13 software metric concepts. The rest of the book gives a thorough handling of the error problem and design of programs, files and inputs (See GILB-RE-76)

Gilb, T., "Data Metrics: A New Major Direction", in IAG <u>Communications,</u> 1/73, and <u>Data Management</u> (USA) Oct. 1972 pp. 35–6, and similarly ACM <u>SIGCSE Bulletin</u> Dec. 1972, pp. 2–3.
These articles are intended as debate starters on the general subject of software metrics.

Gilb, T., "Software Metrics", in <u>Computer Weekly</u> (UK) Sept. 11, 1975, p. 6.
This is a popular article summarizing the practical metrics measurement techniques reviewed in this book.

Gilb, T., "Software Qualities are Measurable", IAG <u>Communications</u> April 1975 p. 9. Similar to the "Software Metrics" article. These articles will not give the reader of this book any new material.

GIRARD-73: Girard and Rault J-C., "A Programming Technique for Software Reliability", in <u>IEEE Symposium on Software Reliability</u>, NY, 1973.
The technique of dual but independent coding, using first APL and then FORTRAN, is examined and the combination with error seeding as a measurement method is examined mathematically. Seeding research is continuing in 1976, according to Rault (private communication) at Thomson-CSF, D.I.B., 33 Rue de Vouillé, F-75015 Paris.

GOULD-72: Gould and Drongowski. <u>A Controlled Psychological Study of Computer Program Debugging</u>. IBM Research Report RC 4083. Oct. 19 1972, 38 pp. The method of seeding bugs into program texts is the primary measurement tool used here to study the effects of different levels of program documentation on the rate and accuracy of logical error identification.

HATTER-71: Hatter, B.J., Excerpt from <u>CCIP Study Regarding Analysis of TRW Software Analysis Data</u>, Lulejian and Associates, Inc., Redondo Beach, California, 1971. An abstract of this is given in TRW-SS-72-04.
Briefly the only significant predictor factor in software cost was the size of the module (of 22 factors studied in 88 routines); however, more than 50 % of variance cannot be explained by size. I note that quality parameters such as reliability, maintainability and portability were not included in the study.

HETZEL-73: Hetzel (ed.), <u>Program Test Methods</u>, Prentice-Hall, 1973 ISBN 0-13-729624-X. Approx. 351 pp.
These are conference proceedings. They are primarily of interest here for <u>Rault's</u> paper describing dual coding. With the exception of a paper from TRW and some comments by H. Mills on measures of complexity, the papers are surprisingly devoid of theoretical or practical metrics. Most of the papers seem to discuss various tools of unmeasured value. A 34-page bibliography is included.

HOARE-72: Hoare, C.A.R. "The Quality of Software", Guest Editorial, in <u>Software - Practice and Experience, Vol. 2,</u> pp. 103-105, 1972. Professor Hoare (Belfast) briefly describes 17 software attributes which he (in 1964, private communication) recognizes as useful for "the design of any engineering product" and here in particular general purpose computer software. No attempt at quantification or numerical measurement is mentioned.

HOSKYNS-73: Implications of Using Modular Programming, by John Hoskyns for Central Computer Agency of the Civil Service Dept. ISBN 0-11-630361-1. 1973. 148 pp. Her Majesty's Stationary Office, London. £ 1.50. A survey report of use of modular programming in the UK.

IEEE-73: Record 1973 IEEE Symposium on Computer Software Reliability. IEEE Catalog No. 73 CHO741-9 CSR, 167 pages. $ 12.

Iresen (ed.), Reliability Handbook. McGraw-Hill, 1966, 692 pp.

Ivanov, Kristo, "Quality Control of Information". On the concept of accuracy of information in data-banks and in management information systems. Doctoral thesis 1972. Royal Inst. of Techn., Dept of Information Processing & Computer Science, FACK, S-104 05 Stockholm, Sweden.

JELINSKI-IEEE-73: Jelinski, Z. and Moranda, P.B. (McDonnell Douglas Astronautics Co.), "Applications of a Probability-Based Model to a Code Reading Experiment", in reference IEEE-73, pp. 78-81. An experiment using bebugging is described.

Jevons, The Principles of Science, Dover Publications, New York, 1958. 786 pp. (originally publ. 1873).

Johnson, Robert R. "Some Steps towards an Information System Performance Theory." Performance Evaluation Review Sept 1972 pp. 4-15. SICCME of ACM. Also publ. in "USA-Japan Computer Conference Oct 1972".

KOHLI-21601: Kohli, O. Robert, High Level Design Inspection Specification, IBM TR 21.601, July 21, 1975, 43 pp.
This report describes the high level design inspection process in detail, and must be seen in connection with LARSON-21586 and FAGAN-21572.

LANGEFORS-THAIS: Langefors, Börje, Theoretical Analysis of Information Systems (THAIS). Studentlitteratur Lund 1966, 1972 and Petrocelli (USA).

LARSON-21586: Larson, Rodney R., <u>Test Plan and Test Case Inspection</u>
<u>Specification.</u> IBM TR 21.586. April 4, 1975, 33 pp.
This report is extensively reproduced in the present text and
in Appendix B. It reports substantial productivity improvements
as a result of error measurement by inspection in the test
planning stages.

LIPOW-TRW-72-09: Lipow, Estimation of Software Package Residual
Errors. TRW-SS-72-09. TRW Systems.
A theoretical, mathematical treatment based on Harlan Mills
(IBM) paper on error seeding as a measurement technique.

Machol (ed.), <u>System Engineering Handbook.</u> McGraw-Hill, 1965.

MILLER-EU-74: Miller, Edward F., Jr. and Paige, Michael R. <u>Automatic</u>
<u>Generation of Software Test Cases,</u> Eurocomp-74 Proceedings
(ONLINE, Uxbridge, UK), pp. 1-12.

Myers: C. D., <u>Composite Design</u>, IBM TR 002406 (see also Myers,
<u>Reliable Software</u>). This technical report attempts to describe
program modularization factors (without actually quantifying
them). The degree and effects of modularization are discussed
without any reference to actual measures. A theory with only
intuitive support for a "good" degree and type of modularization
is described in some detail. The author has the honesty to say
that he does not know the effect of his recommended type of
modularization on many of the attributes of a modularized
system and to list them.

Myers, G. J., <u>Reliable Software Through Composite Design,</u> April 1975,
Petrocelli, N. Y., 160 pp. ISBN 0-88405-284-2. This book is
an extension of Myers's technical report. I have not had the
opportunity to see it.

NAGY-IBM-3407: Nagy, G. and Carlson Pennebaker, M. A Step toward
Automatic Analysis of Logically Undetectable Programming
Errors, IBM RC 3407, June 17, 1971, 25 pages. 1110 program
submissions of PL/I containing 70,000 program statements are
change-analyzed.

NATO, Buxton (ed.), <u>Software Engineering Techniques.</u> April 1970. 164 pp.

NATO/Naur (ed.) <u>Software Engineering</u>, Jan. 1969, 231 pp.

"Performance Evaluation Bibliography", in <u>Performance Evaluation</u> <u>Review,</u> A Quarterly for the ACM Special Interest Group on Measurement and Evaluation, June 1973, pp. 39-49. Although heavily slanted towards hardware performance metrics, this bibliography does contain references to several papers of interest to software metrics students such as Ferdinand (IBM TR 21-476), " A Theory of System Complexity" and Kolence, "Software Physics", to name a couple at random.

RAU-1970: Rau, J., <u>Optimization and Probability in Systems Engineering,</u> Van Nostrand, 1970. 403 pp. A book devoted to calculation of total system reliability, maintainability and availability.

Stamper, R. K., "Some Ways of Measuring Information", <u>The (BCS)</u> <u>Computer Bulletin,</u> Dec. 1971, pp. 432-436.

STUCKI-7208: Stucki, L. G., <u>A Prototype Automatic Program Testing</u> <u>Tool.</u> McDonnell Douglas Astronautics Co. Publication MDAC WD 1985. Also presented at FJCC Anaheim CA, 5-7 Dec. 1972, 25 pages.

STUCKI-750421: Stucki, L. G. and Foshee, G. L., "<u>New Assertion Concepts</u> <u>for Self-Metric Software Validation</u>" by MDAC (McDonnell Douglas) Paper WD2505 March 1975, presented at 1975 Int. Conf. on Rel. Software, April 75, L. A., Calif. 13 pages. The assertion extensions to "PET" software.

STUCKI-750612: Stucki, L. G., <u>The Use of Dynamic Assertions to Improve</u> <u>Software Quality</u> (Research Prospectus), McDonnell Douglas, June 1975. This is an extension of the author's IEEE-73 paper, with measurement of the degree to which the program performs according to "assertions" about its expected actions. It also includes COBOL examples.

STUCKI-IEEE-73: Stucki, L. G., "Automatic Generation of Self-Metric Software", IEEE Comp. Soft. Rel. 73 pages 94-100. (see IEEE-73) Describes instrumentation of FORTRAN programs to measure execution frequency, timing, data values tested.

STUCKI-PET: Program Evaluator and Tester (PET), McDonnell, Douglas M2085074, 1974, 35 pages. Practical manual on use of PET software for FORTRAN program statement execution instrumentation. $2.

Taylor, F. E., "The Protection of Computerized Information Using Cost-Effective Countermeasures". EUROCOMP-74 Proceedings pp. 1007-1021. Risk = size x sensitivity x accessibility. 10-point scales suggested.

THCOS-7309: Proceedings of a Symposium on the High Cost of Software, held at Montery, California, Sept. 17-19 1973, sponsored by USAF Office of Scientific Research, Army and Navy Research. 140 pages. Jack Goldberg, SRI, Editor, SRI Project 3272. This publication highlighted the need for further research into control over software development costs. Specific research areas are systematically identified.

TRW-SS-71-04: Gibson, C. G. and Railing, L. R., Verification Guidelines, A discussion of various software validation criteria, a fore-runner of later TRW work in metrics.

TRW-SS-72-04: Wolverton, R. W., and Schick, G. J., Assessment of Software Reliablity. TRW publication TRW-SS-72-04, Sept. 1972, 28 pp. This is an extremely interesting review of software development methods in space and missile project environments. It contains the results of a study on software cost parameters which is similar to Farr and Zagorski's study (and does not conclude much differently), see HATTER-71. In addition 3 pages are devoted to examples of the use of the bebugging method.

TRW-SS-73-01: Krause, K. W., Smith, R. W. and Goodwin, M. A. Optimal Software Test Planning through Automated Network Analysis, TRW Systems, Redondo Beach CA, April 1973, TRW-SS-73-01, 5 pages. Also presented in Proceedings IEEE Computer Software Reliability Symposium, 1973 (identical papers).

TRW-SS-73-09: Boehm, et al., Characteristics of Software Quality. TRW-SS-73-09, 1973. TRW Systems, One Space Park, Redondo Beach CA 90278, USA. This extensive report was originally prepared for the National Bureau of Standards. It is the first substantial practical attack on the problem of defining and measuring "Software Metrics" on a broad front. It is no longer publicly available. I am deeply indebted to this book and to TRW for the moral and professional support which this report gave, as will be clear from the many references in the present text. On publication of the Software Metrics book, Barry Boehm reported to me that an attempt was being made to make the material available to an international public.

TRW-SS-74-14: Boehm, B. et al., <u>Proceedings of the TRW Symposium</u>
<u>on Reliable, Cost-effective, Secure Software.</u> March 20-21
1974, Los Angeles. By TRW Systems.
Not publicly available at the time of writing, but efforts to
publish it are being made. This excellent seminar documentation
gives details of further work in TRW in the software metrics
field, and is a source of many of the practical examples reported
in the present text. In a sense it is a complete course with
visual aids, in practical software engineering.

WEINBERG-72: Weinberg, G.W., <u>The Psychology of Computer Programming.</u>
Van Nostrand-Reinhold. ISBN 0-442-29264-3., 1972. 288 pp.
Measurements, scientific method and results of Weinberg's own
experiments in programming are features of this book.

Weissman, Laurence M., "A Methodology for Studying the Psychological
Complexity of Computer Programs". Doctoral Thesis, Technical
Report CSRG-37, August 1974. Computer Systems Research
Group, University of Toronto, M5S 1A4 Canada. 231 pp.
This is an excellent example of a serious scientific study using
a series of well-thought-out experiments in an attempt to find
statistically significant correlations between the use of source
program documentation techniques (comments, indentation,
mnemonic variable names and structured programming) and
the resulting measures of productivity and accuracy of the
programmer work. The subjects' personal opinions are
correlated to their test results, which gives us the interesting
insight that programmers are not the best judges of the effects
of new techniques!

Weissman, Carstensen, Fischer and Jørgensen, <u>Experimental Study of</u>
<u>Program Readability and Modifiability</u>, Datalogical Institute,
University of Copenhagen, 1976. Further experiments based
on the previous studies of Weissman and Andersen et al.

Wolverton, R.W. and Schick, G.J., <u>Assessment of Software Reliability</u>,
TRW-SS-72-04, Sept. 1972, 28 pp.

Index

verification of software (TRW-SS-71-04)
viability   145

weighted ranking by levels (= MECCA)   73
Weinberg (maintenance org.)   56,149
Weinberg, G.M., objectives   68
Weinberg's experiments (ref.)   83,257
Weissman   89
Welker, E.L.   137,143,147,194
Wolverton, R.W. (TRW 72 04)

Zagorski, H.J. (Farr)